THE RESPONSIBILITIES OF JOURNALISM

The Responsibilities
of Journalism

ROBERT SCHMUHL, Editor

UNIVERSITY OF NOTRE DAME PRESS
NOTRE DAME, INDIANA 46556

Library of Congress Cataloging in Publication Data

Main entry under title:

The Responsibilities of journalism.

    Papers presented at a conference on the
responsibilities of journalism held at the
University of Notre Dame on November
22-23, 1982 and sponsored by the Center
for the Study of Man in Contemporary
Society in cooperation with the Institute for
Pastoral and Social Ministry.
    Includes bibliographical references.
    1. Journalistic ethics—Congresses.   I.
Schmuhl, Robert.   II. University of Notre
Dame. Center for the Study of Man in Con-
temporary Society.   III. University of
Notre Dame. Institute for Pastoral and
Social Ministry.
PN4756.R47   1984   174'.9097
83-40596
ISBN 0-268-01623-2

PN
4756
R47
1984

Contents

Preface

This book grows out of a conference on "The Responsibilities of Journalism" that took place at the University of Notre Dame on November 22 and 23, 1982. The conference, which was sponsored by the Center for the Study of Man in Contemporary Society in cooperation with the Institute for Pastoral and Social Ministry, explored the moral dimensions of contemporary journalism. The conference sessions sought to broaden the discourse about the ethics and values of journalists and journalism. In addition to considering some principles of moral significance that underlie the behavior of news people, we also wanted to look at the responsibilities journalists have in our democratic society — to themselves, to their institutions, to the subjects they cover, and to the public at large. To enrich this inquiry, we invited ethicists, theologians, philosophers, members of the clergy, business people, and representatives of government to join with print and broadcast journalists, journalism educators, and students in discussing the different aspects of journalistic responsibility. Over 150 people participated.

Christy C. Bulkeley, publisher of the *Commercial-News* in Danville, Illinois, and P. David Finks, a consultant on community affairs from Danville, initiated the idea for the conference by suggesting to Monsignor John J. Egan, who at the time was the director of the Institute for Pastoral and Social Ministry, that Notre Dame would be an appropriate setting for such a national meeting. Ms. Bulkeley, Mr. Finks, and Monsignor Egan were instrumental in launching the project and in providing continuing counsel throughout its development.

The credit for defining the structure and the substance of the conference goes to the steering committee formed by the university to design the conference. Professor David C. Leege, the director of the Center for the Study of Man in Contemporary Society, served as chairman, and J. D'Arcy Chisholm, the assistant director of the Institute for Pastoral and Social Ministry, was the committee secretary. Other members included Harry Kevorkian, director of Telecommunications and Broadcast Standards at WNDU-TV and adjunct associate professor of American studies at Notre Dame; Rev. Edward Malloy, C.S.C., associate provost of the university and associate professor of theology; John J. Powers, managing editor of the *South Bend Tribune*; Robert Schmuhl, assistant professor of American studies, and Rev. Oliver Williams, C.S.C., adjunct associate professor of management. Whatever merit the conference and this book might have is largely due to the work of this steering committee.

The project, however, would not have been possible without the support of the Gannett Foundation of Rochester, New York. A grant from the foundation underwrote many of the expenses for the conference and for the publication of this book. Our appreciation to the foundation, though, goes beyond gratitude for its financial support. John A. Scott, the chairman of the foundation's Board of Trustees, and Gerald M. Sass, the vice-president for education, offered valuable advice and encouragement each step of the way.

Working with the distinguished group of people invited to speak at the conference was truly a pleasure. We are sincerely grateful to Edwin Newman, who delivered the keynote address, and to Elie Abel, Lisa Sowle Cahill, John G. Craig, Jr., Georgie Anne Geyer, Jeff Greenfield, Max Lerner, Robert J. McCloskey, Rev. Edward Malloy, C.S.C., Leonard Silk, John E. Swearingen, and Rev. Oliver Williams, C.S.C., for presenting their remarks and for revising them for publication. Except for the placement of Mr. Newman's keynote address at the beginning of the book, the articles appear in the order in which they were presented at the conference.

We are also deeply grateful to Rev. Theodore M. Hesburgh, C.S.C., the president of Notre Dame, and to Monsignor Egan for the remarks they delivered about the responsibilities of journalism and the university's commitment to continued exploration of the ethics and values of contemporary communications. Their words established the atmosphere for moral dialogue which the conference sought to provide.

Special, personal thanks go to Professor Donald P. Costello, the chairman of the Department of American Studies at Notre Dame. He offered valued counsel and support both before and after the conference. Professor Costello directs a department that has as one of its concerns the study of journalism. This study is conducted within the context of an examination of the entirety of American civilization: its politics, its history, its literature, its fine arts, its economics, as well as its communications system. Such educational breadth enriches the experience of future journalists, and it helped immeasurably in contributing to the interdisciplinary nature of the conference and book.

Thomas Stritch, professor emeritus of American studies, was a valuable source of advice in planning the conference and in preparing the introduction to the book.

Finally, Norma Davitt and Skip Desjardin rendered administrative assistance of great value to the smooth running of the conference. James Powell, formerly the assistant director of Notre Dame's Center for Continuing Education, devoted many hours to making sure that everything was in order. Ann Bromley, Bobbi Thompson, and Marcia Weigle provided secretarial skill deserving of recognition and sincere gratitude.

Introduction: The Road to Responsibility

ROBERT SCHMUHL

In his sprawling yet vibrant autobiography *A Child of the Century*, Ben Hecht describes the satisfaction he experienced when he broke into Chicago journalism in 1910 at the age of sixteen. Noting that "there were no responsibilities beyond enthusiasm," Hecht explains that his first assignment at the *Chicago Daily Journal* entailed acquiring pictures of crime victims for his newspaper. He recalls: "While maturer minds badgered the survivors of the morning's dead for news data, I hovered broodingly outside the ring of interviewers. I learned early not to ask for what I wanted, for such requests only alerted the beleaguered kin, weeping now as much for the scandal coming down on them as for the grief that had wakened them. Instead I scurried through bedrooms, poked noiselessly into closets, trunks and bureau drawers, and, the coveted photograph under my coat, bolted for the street."[1]

After his apprenticeship as a "picture chaser," Hecht began to write "news stories" for the *Journal*. Each effort was an exclusive, he indicates: "Tales of lawsuits no court had ever seen, involving names no city directory had ever known, poured from my typewriter. Tales of prodigals returned, hobos come into fortunes, families driven mad by ghosts, vendettas that ended in love feasts, and all of them full of exotic plot turns involving parrots, chickens, goldfish, serpents, epigrams and second-act curtains. I made them all up."[2] Hecht's technique for scooping the competition was subsequently discovered, and he was suspended without pay for one week. When he returned to his typewriter, Hecht took a "vow to become an honorable and truthful newspaperman." He concludes with a certain restrained pride: "During the twelve years I continued in that calling, I kept my vow, as reasonably as I could."[3]

What Hecht did during his sojourn in journalism came naturally to news people of his era. He, of course, made use of his experience (and his imagination) in creating *The Front Page*, the play he coauthored with Charles MacArthur, which was first produced and published in 1928. Hecht and Mac-Arthur realized from the outset that their picture of journalists in action was both nostalgic and romantic. But the stereotype which their caricatures produced of reporters as cynical, conniving, unprincipled, believing always in the "scoop-is-sacred" idea, became an enduring, at times the defining, image in the popular mind of how journalists went about their work.

The American public swallowed this perception whole. *The Front Page* was a smashing success. Besides the original success in staging the play and its countless revivals, the printed version appears in several editions and collections, and three film treatments of it have been produced, twice with the title *The Front Page* (in 1931 and 1974) and once as *His Girl Friday* (in 1940).[4]

The popular appeal of this view of American journalism notwithstanding, the accuracy of the Hecht-MacArthur portrayal of Hildy Johnson, Walter Burns, and the others (who are, in Hildy's celebrated classification, "a cross between a bootlegger and a whore") is, indeed, questionable, as even the authors admitted. *The Front Page*, in fact, ironically appeared in the wake of far-flung, ground-breaking concern within journalism about the ethical conduct of news people. Four notable book-length studies—Casper Yost's *The Principles of Journalism* (1924), Nelson Crawford's *The Ethics of Journalism* (1924), Leon Flint's *The Conscience of the Newspaper* (1925), and William Gibbons's *Newspaper Ethics*

(1926)—had already appeared, and codes of ethics had been adopted by the American Society of Newspaper Editors (in 1923), by the Society of Professional Journalists, Sigma Delta Chi (in 1926), and by several newspapers and state press associations. Although these embryonic efforts toward the establishment of ethical standards introduced news people to some of the moral questions confronting their craft, the books and codes were greeted with arched eyebrows by numerous editors and reporters. H. L. Mencken, that wise and acerbic commentator on journalism and other aspects of American life, captured the thinking of many of his fellow journalists when he said: "Every time a disabled journalist is retired to a professorship in a school of journalism, and so gets time to give sober thought to the state of his craft, he seems to be impelled to write a book upon its ethics, full of sour and uraemic stuff."[5] Mencken, who had little confidence in "flapdoodlish and unenforceable codes of ethics, by Mush out of Tosh,"[6] interpreted the soul-searching of the twenties as a signal that journalists should use their "common sense" to make improvements in their work.

Mencken's reservations about the books and codes are indicative of the mood at that time of many within journalism and of the reading public. Ruminating on the ethics and responsibilities of the news business was not a popular activity. As a result, the Hecht-MacArthur stereotype, so vividly dramatized, grabbed the public's attention and tended to influence the public's impression of how journalists comported themselves. The picture included such zest, good humor, and bonhomie that their morals seemed beside the point, like those of *The Pirates of Penzance*. Interestingly, within journalism, as the popularity of *The Front Page* and its progeny grew, the institutional interest in the ethics and responsibilities of the news media declined.[7]

What Michael Schudson calls "the ideal of objectivity" directed the thinking and action of reporters beginning in the 1930s.[8] This ideal, in part, developed out of the movement toward professionalism fostered in the growing number of journalism schools and departments. With "objectivity" operating without much internal questioning, news people quite naively assumed that they had to devote little attention to journalistic morality. If we cover the news objectively, editors and reporters seemed to ask, why do we have to worry about issues beyond the stories themselves? The cynicism and hard-boiled detachment so frequently depicted in literary and cinematic renderings of American journalism conformed to the attitudes of many within the press and revealed their reluctance to reflect to any great degree on the motivations or consequences of what they did. But the declining number of daily newspapers—2,008 in 1925 to 1,749 in 1945[9]—and the growth in national news magazines and broadcast networks with news departments resulted in the widespread public perception that large, distant news institutions dictated the information citizens received in ways unlike those of the past. Small, local sources seemed less important. This concern about the changing news media would help to reawaken some of the ethical inquiry that had taken place in the 1920s.

The publication of *A Free and Responsible Press* by the Commission on Freedom of the Press in 1947 caused renewed interest in the moral dimensions of journalism. However, the controversy it provoked, particularly in calling for vigorous self-criticism and for establishment of an independent agency to evaluate the news media, undercut the immediate impact and influence of its worth. The relatively brief report contained so many complaints about the news media and suggested so many different methods for achieving responsibility that a visceral hostility greeted its appearance in some quarters. Robert M. Hutchins, the chairman of the commission, and the other members were criticized, among other things, for not conducting systematic analyses of the press and for not involving journalists more intimately in the deliberations.

The specific suggestions—more access within the news media to opposing viewpoints, the publication or airing of criticism about the media, the establishment of outside agencies to monitor media performance, etc. — and the "social responsibility" theory espoused in the report took several years to take root and to gain acceptance in the thinking of journalists, journalism educators, and the public at large. Ultimately, however, the report was more influential than works that preceded it, and it continues to have meaning today.[10]

Despite the recommendations in *A Free and Responsible Press*, Reinhold Niebuhr, the well-known theologian and member of the Commission on Freedom of the Press, understood the difficulty of achieving individual institutional responsibility within a free and diverse news media. In the introduction to the 1957 edition of *Responsibility in Mass Communication*, Niebuhr observed, "Some over-all philosophy of mass communication is required." He realized, however, that making such a philosophy meaningful to practitioners was anything but simple: "It is difficult to enforce responsible behavior upon the producer, though the theory [of social responsibility] is right in holding the producer morally responsible for the product of news and entertainment in the mass media. It is difficult to compel responsible behavior. On the one hand, while state regulation may be used moderately in the mixed economy which has displaced a laissez-faire economy, regulation is too dangerous in the realm of ideas. On the other hand, securing consumer pressure to police the media is even more difficult than in the case of the market for goods."[11] Niebuhr lucidly defines the dilemma of the "social responsibility" theory and the quandary confronting any effort at news media regulation. A free press is a constitutional right and fundamental to our democratic society. A responsible press is a worthy objective, but largely dependent on how individual journalists and news institutions define "responsible." Outside regulation is unthinkable. Limited, practical mechanisms for fostering and encouraging responsibility and ethical reflection within the media are the only sensible avenues available.

During the 1960s and 1970s, as the news media—particularly television—became a more conspicuous and pervasive force in American life, people in journalism and the public at large inquired with greater frequency about press practices and possible paths leading to more accountability. Press coverage of racial upheavals, the reporting about the Vietnam war, the Nixon-Agnew attacks, the Pentagon Papers case, the disclosures about the Watergate affair, and a host of other situations intimately involving the news media and the subjects they covered placed a spotlight on journalism that made society as a whole consider the messengers and their messages more seriously and more critically. The stakes seemed higher. Sophisticated new technology increased the velocity of communication and increased the quantity of information. With this news explosion came provocative new questions about the role of the media and its impact on our lives. The Hecht-MacArthur stereotype no longer seemed quite so humorous. It required modification. Hildy Johnson, meet Woodward and Bernstein. The cynicism and spirit of competition remained prominent characteristics of journalists, but the wisecracking, "devil-may-care," "damn-the-consequences" attitude of *The Front Page* and its descendants now looked irresponsible and pernicious. Journalism had become more professional, with its practitioners more cognizant of their basic principles, values, and obligations to their craft and to others. The reading, viewing, and listening audience was more educated, discriminating, and aware of the activities and possible transgressions within the news media. Life and death matters affected every neighborhood of what Marshall McLuhan called "the global village"—and we, for better or for worse, were there.

As a result of this new media environment, watching the so-called watchdog became a growth industry with several subsidiaries. People inside and outside journalism who were doing the watching criticized everything, but mostly the specific conduct and practices of journalists and news institutions. Ethical questions concerning such matters as the lack of fairness or balance, the disregard for privacy, the existence of bias, and the glorification of the sensational came to the fore, sparking soul-searching by journalists and head-shaking by the public. Notoriously thin-skinned news people felt criticism coming from many different directions — from journalism reviews, such as the *Columbia Journalism Review*, and from media critics working for other publications or broadcast outlets; from public officials, including presidents and vice-presidents, and from individual citizens provoked to complain; from courts on all rungs of the judiciary ladder and from news councils of all kinds.

This monitoring of the news media that has been taking place since the 1960s has acquainted journalists and the public with ethical questions and with consideration of the media's moral responsibilities. Acquaintance is not necessarily sensitivity, however, nor does it translate into ingrained ethical behavior across the spectrum of journalism. In assessing the current situation, Hodding Carter III, the chief correspondent for the Public Broadcasting System's series on news media criticism, "Inside Story," goes so far as to observe: "To put the matter in plain language, the domain of the mass media today is an ethical jungle in which pragmatism is king, agreed principles as to daily practice are few, and many of the inhabitants pride themselves on the anarchy of their surroundings."[12] The "ethical jungle" does exist, but there are several paths being cut through this jungle that eventually may lead to the road to journalistic responsibility. If these routes are followed and allowed to develop more fully, they will not only help to improve the performance of the news media but will also help to make the news media more accountable to the public, which they attempt to serve.

Codes of ethics: The American Society of Newspaper Editors and the Society of Professional Journalists, Sigma Delta Chi, revised their codes of ethics in 1975 and 1973 respectively. These codes, with their developed lists of standards and objectives, replaced the ethical statements adopted by the two organizations during the 1920s. Such codes are valuable for articulating fundamental principles for conduct in journalism—who can find fault with a line like "Good faith with the public is the foundation of all worthy journalism"?—and for highlighting specific areas of potential difficulty, such as situations involving "any conflict of interest or the appearance of conflict." The codes have limited usefulness, however. They can help to enlighten and to guide, but they lack any means of enforcement.

In the wake of the libel action brought by William P. Tavoulareas, president of Mobil Corporation, against the *Washington Post*, Mobil Oil ran an advertisement in newspapers and magazines across the country in November of 1982 that had as its headline "A Code that needs enforcement." The entire code of Sigma Delta Chi was printed in the ad, probably its widest circulation to date. The primary objective of the message, however, was to drive home the point that, in the opinion of Mobil Oil, the news media had to do more than just have a code. At one point the advertisement stated: "If the media voluntarily adopted and *enforced* this Code, press credibility would rise and the press would be protecting the public from irresponsible reporting."

Voluntary enforcement is a worthy goal; however, Mobil did not offer suggestions as to *how* a news organization should handle transgressions. The code itself includes only general and vague statements regarding enforcement. The "pledge" at the end, for example, says: "Journalists should actively censure and try to prevent violations of these standards, and they should encourage their observance by all newspeople." What "actively censure" means to one person could be a private wrist-slapping; it could mean dismissal to another. Sincere attempts to "prevent violations" might not always work—and, if they do not work, what actions should a news organization take? To talk of enforcement is one thing; implementing it is another and has the faint aroma of regulation.

Codes, though, can help to define and to direct the work of journalists. Making the codes available to all news personnel and conducting discussion sessions about actual situations that bear on matters expressed in the codes are valuable ways to establish awareness and understanding. To its credit, the Ethics Committee of the American Society of Newspaper Editors has attempted to broaden the consideration of the society's Statement of Principles by supporting the publication of *Playing It Straight* (1981). In this short, provocative book John L. Hulteng discusses specific cases and their relationships to the six areas of concern addressed in the statement: responsibility, freedom of the press, independence, truth and accuracy, impartiality, and fair play.[13] Such a work gives life to general statements and enhances the advisory function of the codes.

Internal criticism: Having a neutral arbitrator within a news organization to investigate and to respond to complaints was first tried by the *Louisville Courier-Journal* in 1967. Since that time between forty and fifty newspapers have experimented with full-time ombudsmen or with regular staff members who devote part of their time to evaluating news coverage and to handling the concerns of readers. These in-house critics are responsible for finding out whether a story is accurate, fair, and balanced or whether it has weaknesses that give the public a false impression of the news. The ombudsmen respond to questions and complaints either privately—a call or memo to the reader and the news person involved—or publicly—through a statement of correction or a detailed article about a specific problem or issue. Having an ombudsman can improve a news organization's credibility, because the existence of such a position signals to the public the willingness of the organization to rectify its practices and work. Displaying dirty linen is never pleasant; however, in journalism, it can reduce arrogance and foster greater accountability.

Although relatively few newspapers employ full-time ombudsmen, many of the functions of an in-house critic have been adopted within news departments across the country. Editors are more inclined to devote columns to problems facing a particular newspaper or to the news media in general. Such shoptalk frequently focuses on the difficulties of covering a specific story, and it informs readers about some of the responsibilities and mysterious workings of the press.

A noteworthy new mechanism of internal criticism was begun early in 1983 by A. M. Rosenthal, the executive editor of the *New York Times*, when he instituted a regular column that appears near the space assigned to corrections of factual errors. Called "Editors' Note," the feature "amplifies articles or rectifies what the editors consider significant lapses of fairness, balance or perspective." Explaining why the *Times* began "Editors' Note," Rosenthal commented: "People are astonished by candor. If you say you really blew it, out of some inner desire to say you blew it, the first reaction of a lot of people in our business is 'ah ah, what is he up to?' I'm not up to anything, frankly. The reason we're doing it is it sits well on the stomach. That's all there is to it."[14] Internal criticism done by either ombudsmen or editors achieves two principal goals: news people become more ethically sensitive to potential problems involving such matters as accuracy, fairness, and balance, and the public becomes more aware of the fallibility of the press and journalism's own concern for responsible conduct.

Possibly because of the regulations developed by the Federal Communications Commission, formal mechanisms of internal criticism are much less prevalent in broadcast journalism. However, departments of standards and practices at stations and networks make modest attempts to monitor the collection and production of radio and television news. Interestingly, following the controversy that surrounded the airing of the documentary "The Uncounted Enemy: A Vietnam Deception" in 1982, CBS News created the new position of vice-president for news practices. Van Gordon Sauter, the president of CBS News, likened the new vice-presidency to that of an ombudsman and said that the job involved assessing the fairness and credibility of material after it had been broadcast. The network, though, has done little to inform the public about the existence or work of its ombudsman. Publicizing the efforts of a news organization's in-house critic is an essential component to the success of having internal criticism.

External criticism: Criticizing American journalism, particularly what people perceive to be ethical lapses and transgressions, dates back to colonial times and to the early years of the republic.[15] Until the 1960s, however, serious press scrutiny had an ad hoc quality to it—particular cases or problems were explored, but the endeavor as a whole lacked the sustained, concentrated focus required for continuous, in-depth critical and ethical evaluation. The birth of the *Columbia Journalism Review* in 1961 and the subsequent publication or production of regularly appearing forums of media criticism changed the environment in which journalism operates. Scrutiny of the news media was no longer a one-shot or infrequent exercise by an A. J. Liebling or a George Seldes; it was an ongoing activity that attracted the interest of people inside and outside of journalism.

Each issue of the bi-monthly *Columbia Journalism Review* includes the following excerpt from the founding editorial of the magazine: "To assess the performance of journalism in all its forms, to call attention to its shortcomings and strengths, and to help define—or redefine—standards of honest, responsible service . . . to help stimulate continuing improvement in the profession and to speak out for what is right, fair, and decent." This statement reflects the moral and ethical concern that pervades news media criticism on its various levels. The questions that frame the discourse for analysis of specific cases most commonly revolve around such matters as: Was the coverage accurate and complete? Was the reporting fair and balanced? How was the information gathered? What was the motive of the source of information? What were the consequences of the coverage? Wrestling with these questions affords a critic the opportunity of probing the ethical standards and responsibilities of journalism.

The enormous outpouring of criticism and commentary that surrounded the Janet Cooke case at the *Washington Post* in 1981 vividly dramatized the interest within journalism and throughout the public sector in the issues of credibility and trust. Individual media critics—like David Shaw, Jeff Greenfield, Edwin Diamond, Ben Bagdikian, Thomas Griffith, and Michael Arlen—and established forums of media criticism—such as the *Columbia Journalism Review*, the *Washington Journalism Review*, "Inside Story" on PBS, and "Viewpoint" on ABC—have elevated the inquiry into such matters as the conduct, performance, and effects of print and broadcast journalism. This diverse yet constant stream of analysis and evaluation keeps the fundamental principles of media responsibility in the forefront of the minds of practitioners and the public. When taken seriously, the work of news critics can lead to a reassessment of media practices and to a more enlightened and demanding audience for journalism. The value of such scrutiny far outweighs the expressions of fear and loathing that greeted the recommendation by the Commission on Freedom of the Press of the need for "vigorous mutual criticism."

News councils: Although the concept of an independent agency to evaluate journalistic performance dates back to 1916 with the creation of the Press Fair Practices Commission in Sweden, the interest in establishing news councils did not take hold in America until the late 1960s, when the Mellet Fund for a Free and Responsible Press supported six local councils—in cities as different as Sparta, Illinois (population 3,500) and St. Louis (population 750,000). Aware that such groups "have no real power and can do no more than advise and criticize," the ultimate worth of fostering dialogue between journalists and the public about responsible news media performance was clear.[16] Other councils were established in Honolulu, Louisville, and Boston, and the first statewide council was started in Minnesota in 1971. Two years later, the National News Council was formed. Although opposed by some major news organizations, like the *New York Times* and the Associated Press, the NNC investigated and reported on over two hundred complaints during its eleven years of operation. The National News Council, however, voted to dissolve itself on March 22, 1984.

This voluntary form of self-regulation was useful because it made journalists and certain segments of the public aware of problems and transgressions—some media organizations issued apologies upon the recommendation of the NNC—and it resolved specific cases outside the courts of law. Given that the NNC had no formal or legal authority, it had to rely on the cooperation of the news media in providing evidence about the cases and in publicizing the findings and recommendations of the NNC. Since some news organizations refused to recognize the council's value, its ability to use, in its phrase, "the cleansing light of publicity" was diminished. The National News Council suffered from a lack of visibility and public awareness. At some point in the future, however, news councils on the local, state, or national levels could become significant forces in promoting responsibility and in encouraging professional conduct. When the NNC decided to disband, its president, Richard S. Salant, said: "We believe that a national news council is a valuable and valid idea whose time has not yet come, but will come in the near future—in the best interests of this nation, its press, and its people."

Education: Making news people and the public more sensitive to the responsibilities and moral implications of journalism will have little lasting effect unless the concern becomes firmly rooted in the thinking and action of future reporters, editors, and producers. So much of contemporary journalism involves immediate response that the ethical formation of the individual news person is crucial in deciding how he or she will cover a story. Given the wondrous new communications technology, there is usually little time to consult codes or to consider the commentary generated by internal or external critics about similar situations. What the news person does at the moment will frequently develop out of the moral principles and standards that have been internalized over time.

Describing the workings of the *Chicago Tribune* on the night of the 1983 Chicago mayoral election, Bill Granger, a *Tribune* columnist, wrote:

> If you go to journalism seminars, if you listen to learned profs and pompous editors debate the ethics and morals of modern journalism, you get the wrong idea. That stuff has nothing to do with breaking a story and getting it in the paper. There are only two rules of real newspapering:
>
> Get the story.
>
> Get it out.
>
> All the rest is up to private conscience. . . . You can be one of nature's nobles as a reporter and you can be a low-life, but the litmus test is the same for both of you: Get the story. Get it out.

Later, in the same column, Granger stated: "If you thought *The Front Page* died with the word processor computer, you got it wrong — Ben Hecht and Charlie MacArthur would still be at home on a Chicago paper when a big story is breaking. . . . Everything has changed and nothing very important has changed."[17]

Given this environment, which by no means is restricted to Chicago print journalism, the ethics — the "private conscience" — of the individual reporters and editors dictate the gathering and dissemination of the news. During the past decade, however, educators have devoted much greater attention to developing processes of moral reasoning to guide the activity of news people. The number of college-level classes on journalistic ethics has increased markedly, and schools are more frequently conducting continuing education programs — conferences, meetings, and seminars — that explore issues of media responsibility for practitioners.[18] These educational efforts have considerable potential for positive effect, especially if they help to shape a process for systematic, moral thinking. Establishing a definite, reflective process, such as the one explained in *Media Ethics: Cases and Moral Reasoning* (1983), provides a necessary ethical rationale for the news person.[19] By reflecting systematically on the motivations, techniques, and consequences involved in covering a story, a journalist becomes more fully aware of his or her responsibilities. Such awareness, of course, is an individual matter, but serious long-term educational programs can ultimately lead to institutional sensitivity and action.

Codes, internal and external criticisms, news councils, and education are realistic mechanisms to use in fostering journalistic responsibility. They exist at various stages of development—external criticism of one kind or another flourishes, while the work of news councils lacks widespread awareness and acceptance—and they all require nurturing. There is no single path to the road to responsibility. The different approaches need to intersect and to flow together before journalism will ever arrive at the metaphorical road envisioned here. The paths leading to such a road are diverse because one specific avenue—establishing a system to enforce codes or creating penalty-imposing bodies of peer review—would be impractical and would resurrect justifiable concern about controlling the free flow of information in the United States.

As long ago as 1815, in a letter to James Lloyd, John Adams wrote: "If there is ever to be an amelioration of the condition of mankind, philosophers, theologians, legislators, politicians and moralists will find that the regulation of the press is the most difficult, dangerous and important problem they have to resolve. Mankind cannot now be governed without it, nor at present with it."[20] Adams's sentiment takes on greater meaning in modern, mass-media America—the statement, in fact, is reproduced on the title page of *A Free and Responsible Press*. Adams's idea, however, isn't really worth much consideration. There is an un-American quality to it. The only formal, binding means of regulation that should exist do exist—the legal system and, for the broadcast media, the Federal Communications Commission. But strengthening the various existing mechanisms of self-regulation will help to silence the idealistic and foolish talk about more and different instruments of control. For the sake of freedom and diversity, these mechanisms quite appropriately remain informal methods. Informality notwithstanding, codes, internal and external criticism, news councils, and education can operate together to contribute to an environment within journalism that places ultimate value on ethical responsibilities. If the public perceives that, as a result of these acts of self-regulation, media reports are more truthful, fair, balanced, and sensitive, credibility and trust will follow.

The road to responsibility, to be sure, is not an easy one. Vestiges of the shenanigans that Ben Hecht participated in and that Hecht and MacArthur brought to life in *The Front Page* still exist. They are lamentable yet indigenous to American journalism in all of its rowdy individualism and diversity. Nevertheless, as journalism becomes more professional and as the audience served by the news media becomes more sophisticated and vigilant, acts of irresponsibility will be unmasked for what they are, and they will generate complaints and criticism. This continuing criticism can be both constructive and educational if it helps to produce journalism that is recognized for its commitment to high standards and moral principles. The paths out of the "ethical jungle" await travelers willing to make the journey.

NOTES

1. Ben Hecht, *A Child of the Century* (New York: Simon and Schuster, 1954), p. 123.

2. Hecht, p. 133.

3. Hecht, p. 136.

4. For a discussion of the film treatments of *The Front Page* and of other movies about journalism, see Roger Manvell, "Media Ethics: How Movies Portray the Press and Broadcasters" and Deac Rossell, "The Fourth Estate and the Seventh Art," in *Questioning Media Ethics*, ed. Bernard Rubin (New York: Praeger Publishers, 1978), pp. 209-231 and 232-282.

5. H. L. Mencken, "Learning How to Blush," in *A Gang of Pecksniffs*, ed. Theo Lippman, Jr. (New Rochelle, N.Y.: Arlington House Publishers, 1975), p. 111.

6. Mencken, p. 115.

7. For a discussion of the literature about news media ethics, see Clifford G. Christians, "Fifty Years of Scholarship in Media Ethics," *Journal of Communication* 27 (Autumn 1977), 19-29, and Joseph P. McKerns, "Media Ethics: A Bibliographical Essay," *Journalism History* 5 (Summer 1978), pp. 50-53 and 68.

8. Michael Schudson, *Discovering the News: A Social History of American Newspapers* (New York: Basic Books, Inc., 1978), pp. 3-11.

9. Christopher H. Sterling and Timothy R. Haight, *The Mass Media: Aspen Institute Guide to Communication Industry Trends* (New York: Praeger Publishers, 1978), pp. 19-20.

10. For a discussion of the reception *A Free and Responsible Press* received, see Margaret A. Blanchard, *The Hutchins Commission: The Press and the Responsibility Concept*, Journalism Monographs, No. 49 (Lexington, Ky: Association for Education in Journalism, 1977).

11. Reinhold Niebuhr, "Introduction," in Wilbur Schramm, *Responsibility in Mass Communication* (New York: Harper and Brothers, 1957), p. xv.

12. Hodding Carter III, "Foreword," in Clifford G. Christians, Kim B. Rotzoll, and Mark Fackler, *Media Ethics: Cases and Moral Reasoning* (New York: Longman Inc., 1983), pp. xi-xii.

13. John L. Hulteng, *Playing It Straight: A Practical Discussion of the Ethical Principles of the American Society of Newspaper Editors* (Chester, Conn.: Globe Pequot Press, 1981).

14. H. L. Stevenson, " 'It Sits Well on the Stomach,' " *UPI Reporter*, May 6, 1983, p. 2.

15. For an historical and analytical discussion of press criticism, see Lee Brown, *The Reluctant Reformation: On Criticizing the Press in America* (New York: David McKay Company, 1974).

16. William L. Rivers, "The Dinosaur and His Critics," in William L. Rivers et al., *Backtalk: Press Councils in America* (San Francisco: Canfield Press, 1972), p. 1.

17. Bill Granger, " 'Front Page' Still Lives on Election Night," *Chicago Tribune*, 19 April 1983, Sec. 1, p. 2.

18. For a discussion of educational programs, see Clifford G. Christians and Catherine L. Covert, *Teaching Ethics in Journalism Education* (Hastings-on-Hudson, N.Y.: The Hastings Center, 1980).

19. Christians, Rotzoll, and Fackler, *Media Ethics: Cases and Moral Reasoning*, pp. 1-23.

20. John Adams, *The Works of John Adams* (Boston: Little, Brown and Company, 1856), X: 117.

A Journalist's Responsibility

EDWIN NEWMAN

I have been asked to speak about the responsibility of the journalist. That means that I will be speaking about news.

It hardly needs saying that news is important; if you did not think it was, you would not be here. We in the news business help to provide the people with the information they need to frame their attitudes and to make, or at any rate to authorize or ratify, the decisions on which the well-being of the nation rests. That does not make us part of the system of government. It does not and should not give us any official or semi-official standing. But to the extent that the nation is well-informed or ill-informed, we help to make it so.

I don't mean to sound pompous or ponderous. Most of us in the business are in it because it seemed a pleasant way to make a living, or because of the promise of excitement, or because we were unable to do anything else. But we are in it, and what we do has consequences, for the nation and for the world.

As you might expect, the overwhelmingly larger part of what we do is routine. Try writing stories day after day about consumer prices, or the weather, or the police blotter, or who thinks what at the State Department, and you'll see what I mean. But there are times when you come under unusual pressure, times when you have to move and think fast, times when the business becomes, in a manner of speaking, an adventure. Let's take an example.

People sometimes wonder what it is like to cover the shooting of a president or of some other prominent public figure. The question is sometimes put to me because I have had a hand in anchoring the coverage of the shootings of President Kennedy, Robert Kennedy, Martin Luther King, Jr., George Wallace, and President Reagan. When the shooting of Mr. Reagan took place in March 1981, I was told to get into position in front of a stationary camera in the main newsroom that can be put into action very quickly. It was a matter of picking up my telex and walking the forty or so yards to the camera position. A telex is a device that you wear in your ear, and which is flesh-colored so that it won't distract the audience. Through it you can be fed information from the control room. When you are in position, the idea is to get on the air as quickly as possible. On this day, there was an added incentive to do so, because we could tell from the monitor screens in the news room that ABC and CBS were already on.

This doesn't give you much time to think, except about the information that has come to hand and how you want to phrase it on the air. Later, if there is a pause, other reflections may come along. Disbelief, perhaps. Or sadness about what is happening. But indulging in thoughts like "Not again!" is just to waste time. There is no point in thinking thoughts that cannot be used on the air. Nor is there any point in deploring what has happened. Deploring is too easy. You should be able to say something more valuable and enlightening than that.

One thing you have to work out is how far to permit yourself to comment on the event and whether to stick to the official information. Also, whether to try to weigh the significance of the day's events and to appraise the way those affected are dealing with them. You make these decisions independently at first; as time goes by, and perhaps you are joined on the air by someone else, and assignments are made, and a producer takes charge, it becomes more of a team job. But if you are out front, you cannot escape the responsibility that goes with that; and you will, to a considerable extent, set the tone of your network's coverage.

We were subjected to some criticism of our coverage of

21

the Reagan shooting because we put out some incorrect stories and because we were going along with relatively little information.

A couple of points: We had to go on the air. Shots had been fired at the President. Some of those around him had been hit. You could not not go on the air in those circumstances.

But then we said that the President had not been hit. That proved to be wrong. What about that? The answer is that this information came from the White House. We did not invent it. There was the announcement that James Brady, the White House press secretary, had died. Again, the first word came from someone at the White House. We had no choice but to carry it.

What about the report, on NBC, not on the other networks, that the President was undergoing open-heart surgery? That was an out-and-out mistake by the reporter involved, who apparently heard that the President's chest had been opened to permit surgery, and who somehow turned that into open-heart surgery. We may all wish this had not happened; putting on reports of this kind—by which I mean the airing of information at second hand, or third hand—is the kind of decision people in news sometimes have to make, and sometimes have to make fast.

What about some of the things that I said? Was I not engaging in comment rather than straight reporting? The answer to that is yes, at times, I was. Why? Because it is part of your job, so I have always understood, to put a story in perspective, to offer some sense of its significance and of what its consequences may be.

Whenever something happens of the kind that did happen on March 30, 1981, we ask what we can do to keep it from happening again. What is wrong with our country; why do we have this murderous violence?

I don't pretend to know how to prevent attempts to murder the president, whoever he may be. It sometimes seems that who he is has little to do with it. In a country in which so much gunplay goes on, taking shots at the president is probably only to be expected from time to time. He is written about and pictured and celebrated to excess; great hopes are reposed in him; he is, for some, the source of great disappointments, and he is at times exposed and imperfectly protected.

No doubt it would help if the president attracted less attention, if some proportion were returned to our election campaigns, if our political leaders rose more nearly organically from the system. But these would be the results of changes in our society, not the cause of changes. Maybe the United States is the kind of country that cannot make those changes. Maybe it is so big and so rich, expects so much in the way of entertainment and drama and excitement, and breeds so much success and so much dissatisfaction, that it is firmly set in the direction in which it is now going.

I don't know. But I am quite sure that the presidency, and politics generally, *and* the news business cannot be separated from the rest of American life. They must be, to a great extent, of a piece with it. This is a subject to which I will return.

Is television news fair? It is as nearly fair as any other means of presenting news. In some ways, it is more so. After the Second World War, the British set up a royal commission on the press. One of those called to testify was Lord Beaverbrook, the owner of the *Daily Express*, the *Sunday Express*, and the *Evening Standard*. Lord Beaverbrook was asked why he owned those papers. "To make propaganda," he replied.

Taking the path Beaverbrook did is not open to station or network owners. The airwaves are regulated, and stations must be licensed and must meet certain standards of fairness. Those standards are hazy, but they do exist, and they have some effect.

Moreover, on television, the person appearing may be seen by the public without anyone coming between them or interpreting the one to the other. For example, if you watch one of the Sunday interview programs, you will get a more accurate picture of the views and personality of the person be-

ing interviewed than you will from a newspaper report the next day. That is because it has not been edited. You are not getting only the highlights.

This, of course, raises the question of editing. Most of what you see has been edited. Is that fair? It is a pointless question. With rare exceptions, such as live programs on the air and verbatim interviews in print, editing is unavoidable. It is the essence of journalism. The news, because we are the editors, is what we say it is. That flat a statement sometimes outrages people. But what alternative is there? Who else could or should decide? Not the government, surely. And you cannot go around and take public opinion polls—one of the great bores of the age, by the way—on what to report.

I am not suggesting that what the public wants, or believes it wants, or is led to believe it wants, has nothing to do with our decisions. Nobody puts out a paper with the hope that it will not be read. I would not enjoy the thought that nobody watched me giving the news. Nor could that continue for very long. The line of compromise falls differently from organization to organization. But there is always some compromise.

So how fair are we? Not bad, I think. But it is necessary to understand that what the news is, is not very often determined by considerations of fairness. Obviously, if you carry an accusation against somebody, you have the plain duty to ask him for his comment. Obviously, you should not edit what people say to make them look bad or look good. That will sometimes happen, but you should not try for it. Obviously, you should not allow yourself to be used or manipulated, though that will sometimes happen, also. But the problems are more complex.

In the first place, news is a business, a competitive business. People go into it to make a living. News organizations exist to make profits or, in the case of the television networks, to be part of an operation in which other sectors make the profit. This element of competition has much to do with what *we* do, and it is vital. If we all spoke with one voice, it would be a calamity. But competition does bring about some abuses. It sometimes takes us into hasty reporting that later we have to pull back. It may encourage exaggeration for the sake of a strong lead not justified by the rest of the story. It may result in sheer sensationalism. I remember the headlines that took up the entire front page of the *New York Post* during the Three Mile Island nuclear scare in 1979. The first headline was: "Nuke Cloud Spreading." The second, the next day, was: "Nuke Leak Goes Out of Control." The third day, the headline was: "Race with Nuclear Disaster." The fourth was: "It's Looking Good."

Those headlines were a flagrant example of cheap scare journalism. For most people, that kind of thing is easy to recognize.

There is also the phony story, or partly phony story, such as the one that led to the fiasco of the Pulitzer Prize given to Janet Cooke of the *Washington Post* for the story about the eight-year-old heroin addict. When the story was revealed to be largely fictional and the Pulitzer was withdrawn, there was a good deal of shaking of heads, blushing, heaving of sighs, and drawing of large and momentous conclusions among people in the news business. The *Washington Post* itself ran a 12,000-word article on how it happened.

But it doesn't take anything like that number of words to explain what happened. Competition comes into it, of course, because there is also competition within organizations, by reporters who want to hit the front page, make names for themselves, get ahead. But no institutional safeguards will protect the public against bad reporting. There are only the people in the news business and their competence, wisdom, and honesty. What happened at the *Washington Post* was sloppy work and rotten journalism. The same holds true for the *New York Times* and its phony story on Cambodia—sloppy work and rotten journalism. Why complicate it and elevate it into something more?

We must also consider the CBS documentary in 1982 accusing General William Westmoreland and others of deliberately understating enemy strength in Vietnam. That is now the subject of a lawsuit, and we will have to wait for the outcome, but after *TV Guide* said that the documentary misrepresented the facts, a CBS investigation found many things wrong with the program. The result was that CBS decided to have an additional vice-president, a vice-president for news practices, "to ensure that our organization is fully conversant with CBS news standards and their importance to the credibility of journalism."

What I find barely believable and profoundly depressing is the notion that you need somebody in a news organization to tell others in that organization how to go about doing a fair and responsible job. Is it that much of a mystery? And aren't there people in authority who see to these things?

To return to the consequences of competition, one thing it may lead to is incorrect and premature judgments. It seemed to me that the size of Jimmy Carter's victory in the 1976 New Hampshire primary was exaggerated. It also seemed to me that Gerald Ford's early victories in the 1976 primaries were exaggerated by many news organizations and that Ronald Reagan was written off much too soon. I remember a number of stories along these lines: "What makes Ronnie run?" The suggestion was that Ford had the nomination sewn up and all that Reagan was doing was splitting the party. This was too great an intrusion into the electoral process. It risked influencing voters too much. It was also wrong: Ford probably was helped in 1976 by having a tough opponent he was able to overcome. It gave him greater stature.

Some intervention by the press in the electoral process can't be helped. If you so much as print or broadcast a story about an election campaign, you are intervening. There is no way out of that. But the burden of some of these stories is out of line. In 1980, how many times were Edward Kennedy and George Bush asked when they were going to drop out? Bush never got away from the question.

In the 1982 mid-term election, there was a certain amount

of jumping the gun on election night to be first with this or that projection of the winners. I don't know what is to be done about this: the networks, and other news organizations, are obsessed by polls and polling. In the annals of television, the inventor of the exit poll may take his place with DeForest, Baird, Sarnoff, and Paley.

As I say, I don't know what to do about this. If the instrument is there, we should expect it to be used. But it is a fact that this country is up to its ears in public opinion polls. Most of the time, they are simply boring. They usually labor the obvious, and even when they don't, they can safely be ignored. There is not the slightest reason to believe that American life would be poorer if there were no public opinion polling.

Unfortunately, beyond that, in elections, polls may be dangerous. If candidates want to conduct them, that is their business, though it seems to me that they must push politicians in the direction of telling people what they think those people want to hear, and there is already enough of that. When news organizations conduct them, they lead to public impressions about who is ahead, they establish this or that candidate as "the favorite," and they risk affecting the outcome of the vote. They also help to determine the way in which the outcome will be judged. Why, then, do news organizations place so much emphasis on them? They are easy and they have a semi-scientific aura. I spoke earlier about the herd instinct. Everybody does them, so everybody does them. But they are a poor substitute for reporting. And they are an interference in the electoral process.

Having said that, I would like to add that it is also the case that the government has no business interfering with the press. In the first weeks of the hostage affair in Iran, the administration, through the White House and the State Department, was putting it about that the presence of American reporters and camera crews in Iran was encouraging those who held the prisoners and prolonging the affair. It *is* possible that we overdid the coverage of the daily marches outside the United States Embassy. We overdo all kinds of coverage from time to time. It is a continuing problem in our business, how long you stay with a story, how much prominence you give it, whether—on television—much the same pictures day after day are worth showing.

But it is our job to cover events, not to leave them uncovered. We are not, or ought not to be, in the business of suppressing information. And we would take on a tremendous responsibility if we said that the people of the country were not entitled to see what is going on. These things have to be decided according to the usages of the news business. They can't be decided according to what the government would like.

This question came up again after the failure of the Iran rescue mission. President Carter, at a news conference, asked news organizations "to minimize as severely as possible their presence and their activities in Iran." Given the situation in Iran, the President said, it was his responsibility and obligation to make that request.

The news organizations might have criticized the President's English by pointing out that it is not possible to minimize severely, that the minimum is the minimum, and that is all there is to it. They refrained from doing that, but replied as they might have been expected to, which was that they, too, had a responsibility, which was to cover the news as well as they could. Unless he was naive and badly advised, Mr. Carter could hardly have expected anything else.

Beyond that, would it help the reputation of American news agencies around the world if they appeared to be under a President's orders, or so responsive to his influence? Would it help the reputation of the United States?

There is something else, unpleasant perhaps, to bring up. It was Tuesday, April 1, 1980, the day of the primaries in Kansas and Wisconsin. Early that morning, President Carter announced, on radio and television, that there had been a positive step in the Iranian affair, that the Iranian government had decided to take custody of the hostages. It seemed at the time a pretty bald use of the President's ability to command national air time so as to affect the outcome of the primaries, especially because the so-called positive step faded away to nothing in a few hours. Perhaps news organizations should have minimized their presence when Mr. Carter made that announcement.

Not only do news organizations compete with each other. News is itself competitive, in the sense that any item is competing for air time and newspaper space with every other item. What gets heavy play today might not have yesterday and may not tomorrow, because of other things that are happening. What is news at nine in the morning may not be a minute or two later, because of other things that are happening. That also has to be borne in mind.

I was doing the "Nightly News" when word came in that Howard Hughes had died. Not tremendously important, but we had to get it in. We were about eight minutes into the show. Think of what went on in the control room to rearrange that program.

I go into this to emphasize that, in a sense, news is an accidental business. Much of what we do results from that, and from pressures of time.

News is also a matter of habit, of stereotype. I mean by this that we are in the habit of looking for it where we have usually found it, and of reacting to it and judging it in the way that we usually have. One result of this is that we do not always understand new developments quickly enough. The rebelliousness among blacks in the 1950s and 1960s we took a long time to catch on to. We overestimated some black leaders who turned out not to be leaders at all. We did not quickly enough understand the revolt on the campuses at the time of Vietnam, and we certainly did not understand the unfavorable reactions to that revolt off the campuses. News organizations generally did not understand the war in Vietnam for a long time and treated it as another G.I. Joe experience. It wasn't. Few wanted to believe that it was as foolish and cruel an undertaking as it was.

A related matter: What is news on television often depends on where your reporters and cameramen are. If you keep people at the White House, you will be tempted to use stories from there, if only for economic reasons, and also because the people you have there are not somewhere else, covering something else. If you send reporters and camera crews on a trip with the secretary of state, you tend to use what they send back. If you staff a story day after day, you will have it on the air day after day. If you find little interest in a certain kind of news, foreign news, say, you won't use it. And if you don't use it, you discourage interest in that kind of news and create a bias against it.

I said that what is news may depend on where your reporters and camera crews are. In my opinion, a good deal of the film we use is not worth using, and when there is interesting film, we rarely show enough. But we are in the picture business, and we are influenced by the existence of good pictures, or their absence. This has much to do with the amount of time we assign a story in a news program.

A question that often comes up has to do with what is called instant analysis. I have done a great deal of that, so I feel qualified to say something about it. Instant analysis, in my view, is just reporting. All you are doing is saying, This is what he said, or she said. This is what is important. This is what the implications and consequences may be. You would be doing that if you worked for a paper or a wire service, and you would be doing it against a deadline. It may be slightly more difficult on television, but it is not different in kind. To which I should add that nobody is obliged to listen to it. We can be switched off and no doubt often are.

I would hate to give the wrong impression. We are, on the whole, fair. What I have been trying to say is that the problems are not what they are so often made out to be — the products of bias. They would be much easier to deal with if they were.

How do reporters distinguish between fact and rumor? Let's take a few examples from my own experience where fact and rumor had to be judged by those on the spot. In 1958, the Roman Catholic College of Cardinals was choosing a pope. I was one of the NBC men on the colonnades in St. Peter's Square at the Vatican, waiting for the white smoke to go up to tell us that a pope had been chosen. It went up, and the NBC correspondent I was working with announced that it had. Everybody reported that it had—except one man, who happened to be Winston Burdett of CBS. To Winston, an old hand in Rome, the smoke looked grey. He was right. My colleague and I were alternating on the air, so it fell to me to say that no pope had been elected. I remember the words I used: "There is no pope. There is no pope." I am not criticizing my colleague. In his position, I would have done what he did. We had a priest working with us. The smoke looked white to him, too.

These things happen. You're in a rush. You're in competition. And sometimes you simply make a mistake.

Let's take another example: the shooting of President Kennedy. When I heard about it, at lunch, I ran back to the office. We were on the air with it on television but not on radio. I was assigned to radio, but before I was, I stood around the newsroom and, as it happened, picked up a phone that rang. It was a member of our camera crew in Dallas. He said that President Kennedy was dead. I asked how he knew. The Secret Service had told him, he said.

I told the then president of NBC News about this. He spoke to the man in Dallas and decided not to go on the air with it. He would not, he said, announce the death of a president unless it was official. The result was that CBS beat us by thirty minutes, because when Dan Rather reported that Mr. Kennedy was dead, CBS decided to go with him. I do not criticize CBS, and I do not criticize the NBC executive who made the decision he did. Both decisions were defensible.

News is, to say the least, not an exact science. During the Three Mile Island scare, a bulletin came up on the United Press International wire quoting a spokesman for the Nuclear Regulatory Agency as saying, "There exists the ultimate risk of a melt-down." I was told to go on the air, break into the program then on — this is called a network interrupt — and give the news. I looked at the bulletin, decided that I did not know what its significance was, and suggested to the head of NBC News that we wait. He agreed.

We waited, and while we did, ABC and CBS went on with the bulletin, explaining it as well as they could. We put in a call to the Nuclear Regulatory Commission and after a good deal of trouble, got some information about what the ultimate risk of a melt-down meant. It meant much less than might have been thought. When I did go on, we were able to put the story into perspective. It was less scary than it had originally sounded. But, of course, we were the third network to get on.

I don't say this to criticize the opposition. They went one way, we went another. I keep coming back to the same point: Somebody has to make these decisions. There is no way out of that. What matters is how well the decisions are made, whether those who make them are qualified to do so. There cannot be certainty and uniformity in the news business. That is not the kind of undertaking it is.

I think the key to the whole thing lies here: It is easy to state general principles. It is easy to talk about the noble undertaking of journalism. The real questions are: How good are we? How competent are we? And is there a demand in the United States for first-class journalism?

I don't want to argue that there was a golden age of American journalism, which coincided with my first twenty or thirty years in the business. It is not unheard of for older people to complain that the younger people coming along aren't up to much. Still, there has been a change: Television is not the same as newspapers: it puts more emphasis on personality and on presentation, on the cosmetic. It calls for a different kind of writing. It does not often require the extended exposition of ideas or the elaboration of fairly complicated arguments. It tends to turn journalists from outcasts, or at any rate, outsiders, into public figures, heroes, merchants of charm. I am overdrawing the picture, of course, and certainly there are people in television news who are first-rate and who would have been first-rate in other branches of journalism. Indeed, some of them were, before they went into television.

Still, the larger tendency is there. I spoke earlier about competition in our business. There now appears to be a competition, on television news programs, in wishing the viewers well. They are urged to have a good day, have a good night, have a good weekend, have a good week. They are told to enjoy, to be well, to take care, to take good care. A local New York anchorman signs off: "We do care about what happens to you."

What has this to do with news? And why aren't "Good morning," "Good evening," and "Good night," which are required by simple courtesy, enough? I'm not suggesting that those of us who are on the air ought to be snarling at the viewers, but why this competition in fulsomeness?

This is not a small matter. Indeed, it symbolizes what is happening to our business, which is more and more the province of people who have had no, or next to no, experience as journalists in this country or abroad. There is confusion about what we are. Television is peculiarly personal, far more personal than newspapers can be. This must affect the conduct of those who appear on it. But we ought to be clinging to such detachment as we can, not surrendering it.

In that connection, on election night, November 2, 1982, Dan Rather on CBS kept urging viewers, who lived where the polls had not closed, to vote. This is not, or should not be, the concern of news broadcasters. For one thing, the size of the turnout in an election may help to determine the outcome of that election. We have no right to intervene in that. In any case, it is not for newsmen and newswomen to urge people to vote. That is for the editorial writer, perhaps. For the rest of us, whether people vote is something to report and weigh, not deplore or cheer.

Speaking of that election night, a few of its more ironically amusing moments came in the accounts of the money spent in a number of contests. Some of those accounts were given by men and women who, themselves, are paid tremendous salaries for reading a few lines of copy, and who employ agents to negotiate those salaries and other terms of their contracts, including guarantees of appearances on particular programs, the services, in some cases, of hairdressers, and so on.

As I say, I found that ironic. It also has the ring of false naiveté about it. Big money is almost everywhere in American life. It doesn't distort or influence politics any more than it does many other things. Look at sports, and the National Football League strike of 1982.

It is the application of the techniques of public relations and advertising to the political process that costs so much. And the application of these techniques helps to determine the sort of product that emerges in politics, just as it does elsewhere, including the news business, in which so much viewing with alarm is being done.

When we engage in that viewing with alarm, we ought to bear this in mind, that politics cannot be insulated from the rest of American life. Whether insulating it would be a good idea is debatable, but in any event, it is not possible. To change American politics, we will have to change much more than American politics. It seems to me to be the responsibility of anyone who calls himself a journalist to understand that.

I would like to speak now about what I take to be another responsibility of the journalist, which is to know something about the English language. Many do not meet that responsibility. CBS told us not long ago about someone who had been not merely strangled, but strangled to death. Anyone undergoing that process would then not be a "living survivor." That also came from CBS.

The *New York Times* reported that Israel annexed the Golan Heights without "prior warning to the United States." Maybe the Israelis intended to warn us about it afterward.

Cable News Network referred to John Hinckley's "self-proclaimed historical deed." They should have said historic, and they should have said proclaimed. Self-proclaimed means the deed was talking about itself. I have heard on television news programs about a "self-confessed murderer," as though somebody else could confess for you. *Time* magazine has used the phrase, "successfully persuade." The *New York Times* has used "successfully capture," "successfully conceal," and "successful rescue." Can people be unsuccessfully persuaded, or someone unsuccessfully rescued?

Oh well, someone will say, that is Newman, the crank about language, the elitist. All right. Let's take less abstruse examples. A correspondent on ABC said, "That may sound like a lot of money to you and I." A few days before the funeral of Leonid Brezhnev, NBC's "Today" show announced, "Brezhnev will lay in state." The *Oklahoma Journal* ran a photograph of a nurse with the physician "in whom's office she worked."

The paper in Bradenton, Florida noted with gratitude that the avocado country in that state had been "spared a hurricane's wrath," r-a-t-h; Cable News told us about a July day that was a scorcher, s-c-h-o-r-c-h-e-r; the *Washington Post* spelled incidentally i-n-c-i-d-e-n-t-l-y and foreseen f-o-r-s-e-e-n.

I sometimes think that we are entering an age of incoherence. A good deal of what is said on television news programs make no sense at all. Try this one: "Reaction to the P.L.O. met with guarded reaction tonight." Here's another: "If you are among the millions of New Yorkers who spend a lot of time waiting for buses, you are not alone." On a New York station, I heard about someone who was "pointing the guilty finger at Israel." Pointing the guilty finger. Do these people know what they're saying?

I think that there are fewer and fewer people in the news business who know the difference between what is correct and what is incorrect. The word Arabist is now being used to designate someone who favors the Arab side. It means someone who has specialized in the study of Arabic languages and culture.

We have reached the point where, when somebody is quoted in print as making a mistake in English, we can't know whether he made it or the paper did. The *Chicago Tribune* quoted the general manager of the Chicago Bears as saying, after the player draft, "We did get less immediate help from this draft than we might of." Did he say "might of" or did he say "might have," with the reporter thinking "might of" was correct. Nowadays, how can you tell?

Sometimes you cannot believe your eyes and ears. The Springfield, Missouri *News Leader* invented a word: delightment. The *New York Times* invented one: destroyal. And a second one: equanimously. The *San Antonio Express News* invented another: fewness. The Baton Rouge, Louisiana *State-Times* carried a picture of a gunman—sometimes known as an armed gunman—leaving a bank with a sack of money while "frightful" customers lay on the floor.

This is—believe me—a tiny sample.

There are a few other points I would like to make.

The news business builds people up and then acquires an interest in tearing them down. We go through this periodically—with John Kennedy, Lyndon Johnson, Robert McNamara. We help to create expectations that cannot be realized; then we do stories about the wreckage that follows.

When this happens, the public figure involved often has trouble figuring it out. He may think that he is being unfairly treated, picked on, that he is the victim of a conspiracy, or that there is a heavy bias against him. President Johnson came to believe that the press was against him. So did President Nixon. So did President Carter. President Reagan, so far as we know, has not reached that point, apart from his complaints about some reporting of economic matters, stories about people being thrown out of work, that sort of thing.

You may remember his celebrated reference to some fellow out of a job in South Succotash somewhere.

We have, nonetheless, seen with Mr. Reagan the buildup that may lead to the disillusioning later on. For a while, you will recall, you couldn't get through a day without being told that Mr. Reagan was a great communicator and that he used television uncommonly well. Which of course he does. He is comfortable in front of a camera, as, after all, he ought to be.

But the fact is that a communicator cannot be separated from what he communicates. And the public has to be receptive. It was a lot easier to put over budget cuts and tax cuts in the spring of 1981 than it was for Richard Nixon to put Watergate to rest, or for Lyndon Johnson, near the end, to convince the American people that Vietnam was not an act of folly.

It may be dangerous to a president to have the idea around that he was a great communicator. That kind of thing can set up a reaction and put people on guard. Such ideas are, however, the easy currency of journalism. You have the story this day that someone is a great communicator, and soon after you have the story that well, maybe he isn't. Two for the price of one.

I hope that it will be understood that presidents and their families are not required to be clever, witty, handsome, or even interesting. If they happen to be, well and good, but for the most part, they ought to be taken in stride, for their own sake and for the health of the nation. We ought to understand that a president is a man — and when the time comes, a woman — who has a job to do, a political job, and as far as possible ought to be judged on that and that alone.

I see some danger in the yearning for leadership in the United States, the desire to have a new man take over, inspire us, and bring out our best. We do have a presidential system. But it is too easy to believe that the only source of dynamism and leadership in the country is the White House. It is also dangerous, as the Nixon, Johnson, and Kennedy administrations, to go back no farther than 1961, demonstrate. We have to avoid idolatry, unrealistic expectations, and disproportionate disappointments.

In connection with all of this, I am beginning to wonder whether it is logical to expect to have a level of political life generally that is much higher than the broad level of popular culture in the country.

The kind of politics we have probably cannot be divorced from the kind of education we have, the kind of newspapers we have, the television and radio we have. It cannot be separated from our way of doing business and from our reliance on the techniques of advertising and public relations and market surveying. That is why we see so little spontaneity. We are putting politics — at any rate, presidential politics — out of bounds to anyone who is not prepared to be managed and groomed or turned into an ingredient in a recipe.

If that is true of politics, it is also true of the news business. You should not expect the news business to operate at a much higher level than the rest of society generally. Of course, there is a range of competence, of integrity, of intent. Not everybody aims at the same audience. But by and large, the mass-circulation papers and magazines and television stations and networks will reflect the level of popular culture. If we want to raise that level, we must recognize that the amount and quality of the information the American people receive is important. It is a serious matter, to be treated seriously. Not lugubriously. Not without humor. But seriously.

What worries me about television news, as I have said, is not bias. Where that does exist, it is a minor problem. What counts is the level of competence, the knowledge, the experience with which the news of the day is approached. Breeziness is not a substitute for those qualities. Hair, real or tacked on, is not a substitute. Smiles don't make up for the absence of judgment. Being told to have a good day or a good night, or to "Enjoy," is less valuable than getting the information you need.

I want to say, in closing, how I think television news can be improved. *We* can do it, of course, within limits. As I've tried to indicate, there are many factors at work in the news business. Not everybody in it is pleased with the way it is going. But what *we* do is aimed ultimately at the public, from which it follows that pressure for improvement from the public could be important. There are many calls on people's time. And the primary responsibility is ours. It is our business. But one safeguard against biased and incompetent reporting is for the public to know more about the news business than it does. I believe that the American people are entitled to know more, so that they can better judge what they get, so that they can understand that news is not a uniform product, that it is not uniform even within individual organizations, like NBC News. I believe that there is not nearly enough criticism of us, not nearly enough understanding of how we work, of why we do what we do, and of how powerful our habits and stereotypes are.

We in the news business have to be skeptical about what we're told; that goes with the job. If people are skeptical about what they get from us, that is a very good thing. At least, it is a beginning.

What, then, is the responsibility of the journalist?

It is to be a journalist.

That may sound sententious. It is sententious. But what I mean is to be a competent, qualified journalist. That is not easy. There are many forces working against it. Very many. And strong. But that is the job.

Hutchins Revisited: Thirty-five Years of Social Responsibility Theory

ELIE ABEL

Our story begins on a December day in 1942. During a meeting of the directors of Encyclopaedia Britannica, Henry Luce passed a note to Robert Hutchins, chancellor of the University of Chicago, asking what it would cost to conduct a survey of the American press. Hutchins replied, "$60,000 a year until finished."[1] What Luce had in mind was an inquiry into the "present state and future prospects of freedom of the press." His motives, variously interpreted by others, were defined by Luce himself in these words:

> What was uppermost in my mind were my own troubles as Editor or Editor-Publisher. I thought I knew enough about the nature of things to know that the troubles of my occupation were related to philosophy and morals — even more directly than is the case with most occupations. Furthermore I was aware . . . that the contemporary world of thought and moral philosophy was in a somewhat acute state of confusion and that therefore "correct" answers to philosophical and moral questions of the day were not readily available but could be supplied, if at all, only by the very best philosophical talent and effort.[2]

Hutchins lost no time following up. Time, Inc. contributed $200,000; Encyclopaedia Britannica chipped in $15,000 more, and the Commission on Freedom of the Press, better known as the Hutchins Commission, started its inquiry. There were thirteen members, mostly academics, headed by Hutchins himself. The commission's first volume, titled *A Free and Responsible Press*, was published on March 27, 1947, and promptly denounced by all but a handful of newspapers. With remarkably few exceptions, editors and publishers depicted the report as a blueprint for government regulation of the press. Luce was not proud of his handiwork. He denounced the report for what he called its "appalling lack of even high school logic." More predictably, Colonel Robert McCormick of the *Chicago Tribune*, said he would not take the time to read "the outpourings of a gang of crackpots."

In fairness it must be said that the commission was hardly advocating a system of federal mind control. It called for action by the press itself to correct certain of its perceived shortcomings. The Hutchins Commission report did see an important role for government to play, but it was no less aware of the dangers that course might entail: "Government ownership, government control, or government action to break up the greater agencies of mass communication might cure the ills of freedom of the press, but only at the risk of killing freedom in the process."

For a good many years before 1947, the press had been widely faulted for lack of what we have come to call "social responsibility." Theodore Peterson's useful compilation of perceived shortcomings, as cited by various twentieth-century critics, makes these points: That the press:

(1) Has wielded enormous power for its own ends. Its owners have propagated their own opinions, especially in matters of politics and economics, at the expense of opposing views;

(2) Has been subservient to big business and at times has allowed advertisers to control editorial content;

(3) Has resisted social change;

(4) Has often paid more attention to the superficial and sensational than to the significant in its coverage of current happenings;

(5) Has endangered public morals;

(6) Has invaded the privacy of individuals;

(7) Is controlled by one socio-economic class, loosely described as the "business class," which makes access to the press difficult for newcomers and thereby endangers the free and open market of ideas.[3]

That bill of particulars is being drawn and redrawn to this day. The American Right has its favorites on that list; so also does the Liberal-Left. On certain particulars, the Left and the Right tend to agree: that the press, now transmogrified into a strange abstraction called the media, wields enormous power, that it continues to elevate trivia at the cost of substance, that it still invades the citizen's privacy more or less at will. Yet some, at least, of the enduring complaints ring hollow today. The Right, for example, is likely to argue that the media accelerate social change, rather than resist it; that in the post-Vietnam era, far from being subservient to business interests, they are often hostile to those interests. Shifts in popular perception are difficult to calibrate, all the more so if one attempts to trace a cause-and-effect relationship between the Hutchins Commission report and what I perceive to be certain beneficial changes since 1947 — and even more markedly since the uproar of the sixties — in the performance of American newspapers.

The Hutchins Commission laid down a new agenda for the press, a set of standards, if you prefer, that warrant a second look some thirty-five years later. First, that the press ought to provide "a truthful, comprehensive, and intelligent account of the day's events *in a context that gives them meaning.*" On this point the press has not filed a dissent. In fact the goal of accuracy, of striving to discover and disseminate the truth about public affairs, was not invented by the Hutchins Commission. It is — and has been for several decades past — part of the journalist's conventional wisdom. Fact and opinion are separated in most American newspapers. Objectivity, as Peterson points out, was no longer a goal of the press back in 1947; it had become a fetish.[4]

Truth is harder to pin down, however, than the commission may have imagined. "It is no longer enough to report, the *fact* truthfully,"the commission held. "It is now necessary to report *the truth about the facts*." Here the terrain becomes more rugged and the progress of the press somewhat labored. The press is exhorted to evaluate the truthfulness of conflicting sources, not merely to report, for example, that one source said supply-side economics will lift the United States out of the current recession, while a second source said that was voodoo economics. A controversy of this nature has little to do with facts. It is a matter of opinion, and it seems to me unrealistic to ask of the press that it coolly adjudicate disputations among economists. There is merit, however, in the suggestion that facts need to be placed in a context that gives them meaning. Most journalists would agree that merely setting down the facts is not enough, and I see encouraging signs that increasing numbers of newsmen today work hard at reconstructing the essential context of events they are reporting.

A second requirement laid down by the Hutchins Commission was that the press must serve as "a forum for the exchange of comment and criticism." It appears to mean that newspapers, news agencies, and other media should try to present all significant viewpoints on public issues, including viewpoints that happen to be unpopular or in conflict with their own. In this area the American press has, I believe, made appreciable progress since the Hutchins Commission report. The increasing popularity of Op-Ed pages is one benchmark. Another is the spreading notion that newspapers ought to apply the common-carrier principle in their operations: No more than a railroad has the right to refuse to carry any passenger with the price of a ticket should a newspaper refuse space in its news columns for the actions or viewpoints of groups or individuals it may choose to denounce on the editorial page. There is irony in the circumstance that acceptance of this common-carrier doctrine owes something to the spread of chain or group ownership, a trend that greatly concerned the Hutchins Commission. I am not, by any stretch of the imagination, an advocate of chain journalism. But there is plenty of evidence that monopoly publishers in this age of one-newspaper cities are far more sensitive than they were, say, thirty years ago to their civic responsibilities. This is not to say that monopoly publishers have openly embraced the social responsibility theory; only that in the words of John L. Hulteng, "when there is only one game left in town, it must be an honest one."[5] We have, after all, come a fair distance from the attitude attributed to William Peter Hamilton of the *Wall Street Journal*, that "A newspaper is a private enterprise owing nothing whatever to the public, which grants it no franchise. It is therefore affected with no public interest. It is emphatically the property of the owner, who is selling a manufactured product at his own risk."

The commission's third standard—that the press has an obligation to project "a representative picture of the constituent groups in society"—remains a problem area to this day. What the Hutchins Commission had in mind was a voluntary undertaking by the press to portray more faithfully than in the past the true condition and aspirations of such ethnic minorities as Blacks, Hispanics, and Asians. Here, as well, there has been progress, fitful progress at best, powered by external events and pressures rather more than by the conscience of the news industry: the civil rights campaigns of the sixties, affirmative action programs in federal and state governments, ghetto riots in some of our biggest cities. For the media, the pressure became most intense when, in 1968, President Johnson's Commission on Civil Disorders reported:

> The communications media have not communicated to a majority of their audience, which is white, a sense of the degradation, misery and hopelessness of living in the ghetto. They have not communicated to whites a feeling for the difficulties and frustrations of being a Negro in the United States.

The response of some media was to hire black reporters; special training programs for minority journalists were started at Columbia University and later at the University of Califor-

nia; journalism schools were able to raise money for minority
scholarships, and a handful of minority journalists already
employed won swift promotions. But few of the foundations
that supported this effort were prepared to stay the course.
When, for example, I approached one foundation executive,
asking that he extend his support grant for minority fellow-
ships at Columbia into a third, or perhaps it was a fourth,
year he replied: "Haven't we done enough? I thought you'd
have the problem cleaned up by now." Well, we haven't
cleaned it up, not yet. According to one published estimate,
close to two-thirds of the country's 1,750 newspapers do not
have a single minority reporter or editor. Some 99 percent of
all editors and broadcast station managers are white. And,
although ethnic minorities account for 17 percent of the population, only 4 percent of media employees at all levels be-
long to those minority populations.[6]

We have seen over the past three decades certain offsetting
gains in media sensitivity. These are hard to measure, admit-
tedly, but it is my impression as an inveterate newspaper
reader and occasional television watcher that the grosser
forms of racial stereotyping the Hutchins Commission hoped
to see eliminated are few and far between these days. The old
problem of race and class in America seems to me to have
taken a new form with the flight to the suburbs of our mostly
white middle class, precisely the class that editors and, of
course, advertisers want to reach. The term "inner city," come
to think of it, no longer defines a geographical area. It evokes
poverty, crime, drugs—a dangerous place inhabited chiefly
by Blacks and Hispanics. The purchasing power, of course, is
out in the mostly white suburbs, and some of our most
respected metropolitan newspapers—from the *New York
Times* in the east to the *Los Angeles Times* in the west—tailor
their product increasingly for that suburban readership. As
the publisher of the *Los Angeles Times* has argued, "it would
not make sense financially" for his paper to expand its
coverage of low-income minorities because, he said, that au-

dience "does not have the purchasing power and is not responsive to the kind of advertising we carry."

One more Hutchins standard — that the press ought to provide "full access to the day's intelligence" — warrants special attention today, because it is notably in this area that the commission's reports have foreshadowed the shape of things to come. Access is the heart of the matter, access *for* the press to the government's store of information so that the press, in turn, may provide its audience with access to "the day's intelligence."

Although most of the press remained hostile to the Hutchins recommendations, some years before the commission published its first report, press people had been developing a new doctrine called "the people's right to know." The phrase was coined in 1945 by Kent Cooper, then general manager of the Associated Press. His primary interest at the time was in breaking down the barriers to free international communication. By 1953, the doctrine had been naturalized in the pages of a book titled *The People's Right to Know*, by Harold Cross, a libel lawyer who taught me what little I know about the ways in which newspapers wind up as defendants in the courts. "Public business," Cross wrote, "is the public's business. The people have the right to know. Freedom of information is their just heritage. Without that the citizens of a democracy have but changed their kings."[7]

Cross saw freedom of information as the foundation stone of all First Amendment freedoms. In its absence, he argued, other freedoms were necessarily at risk. He believed that citizens must have a legal right to information concerning actions taken by government in the name of those citizens. The Cross doctrine troubles many constitutional lawyers to this day. They will tell you that there is no such right, implicit or explicit, as "the people's right to know." The formulation, they say, has more to do with moral philosophy than with law. Yet the campaign triggered by Cooper and Cross, reinforced by the dogged lobbying of the American Society of

Newspaper Editors, the American Newspaper Publishers Association and other professional groups, was to culminate in passage of the federal Freedom of Information Act and literally dozens of "sunshine laws" adopted by state legislatures around the country.

That was a breakthrough, though hardly a decisive victory. Witness the recent efforts of the administration and Congress to water down the Freedom of Information Act. Tradition was on the side of those legislators and officials who wanted to turn the clock back. Officials in every country I know anything about, our own included, feel a great deal more comfortable clutching their secrets to their bosoms than being forced to disclose them. For more than 150 years, Washington officialdom cited in defense of this attitude a housekeeping act of 1789 authorizing federal department heads to adopt regulations for "the custody, use and the preservation of records, paper and property." The Administrative Procedure Act of 1946 eased matters somewhat, but it authorized federal agencies to limit access to official records "for good cause" or when the public interest was served by denial. The right of access to legislative and administrative proceedings, as Cross noted, was a concept of "strikingly modern origin." Thus there were no reporters present when the framers debated the American Constitution, and for many generations reporters have been attending sessions of the House and Senate as a matter of courtesy, not legal right.

Today the concepts of citizen and press access to government documents and to open meetings of public bodies are still questioned in the courts, but the Congress, over the past fifteen years, has been more forthcoming. In passing such legislation as the Privacy Act of 1974, the Government in Sunshine Act, the Family Educational Right and Privacy Act, and the Fair Credit Reporting Act, successive Congresses have extended the right-to-know principle beyond the expectations, I would guess, of Cooper or Cross or Hutchins. Even the courts, in such landmark decisions as the Pentagon Papers case of 1971 and more clearly, in the Red Lion case of 1969, have upheld the right-to-know principle. Neither the Congress nor the Federal Communications Commission was entitled to abridge the right to free speech, the Supreme Court ruled in the Red Lion case, adding that the right belonged to "the people as a whole."

"It is the right of the viewers and listeners, not the right of the broadcasters . . . (the right of the public) to receive suitable access to social, political, aesthetic, moral and other ideas and experiences which is crucial here," the Court ruled, in upholding an FCC regulation that requires broadcast stations to provide an opportunity for reply to individuals and groups whose character or integrity had been attacked—in this case by a small radio station in Red Lion, Pennsylvania.

Access had become a fighting word, access *for* the media to the processes and documents of government—as the media owners and managers would have it—and access *to* the media—as articulated by a few legal scholars and many young journalist-advocates of "democracy in the newsroom." Much of the steam has gone out of that movement since the late sixties. But media managers, while rejecting the notion of public access to the media as a First Amendment right, have somewhat defensively begun to show a sharpened sensitivity to complaints about unfair, incomplete, or distorted reporting.

Some newspapers, more than thirty by the latest unofficial count, have appointed ombudsmen to investigate reader complaints and to survey, often in sharply critical tones, the performance of their colleagues. The National News Council, established in 1973, opened another avenue of media accountability. It is an independent, nongovernmental organization which receives and investigates complaints from the public regarding fairness and accuracy, in addition to publishing occasional studies of press performance. The council has no enforcement powers, save the power of exposing instances of shabby performance by the media. In the spirit of full disclosure I must confess to membership in the council, which to the surprise of many skeptics is about to celebrate its tenth birthday. Yet some of our most prestigious news-papers still refuse to cooperate with the council or to publish its reports, presumably on the theory that if they ignore it, the pesky thing will wither and die.

The council will survive, I believe, in spite of its detractors. The Hutchins Commission, incidentally, proposed the estab-lishment of some such agency to appraise and report on press performance each year. But the council has a broader man-date and is no longer widely perceived as any kind of threat to press freedom. [This essay was written before the National News Council voted to dissolve itself on March 22, 1984. —Editor's note.]

To conclude, then, the social responsibility theory of the press, first enunciated in a coherent fashion by the Hutchins Commission, is, even after thirty-five years, alive and well. In some respects it has fallen short of Dr. Hutchins' expecta-tions; in others it may have surpassed them. If it remains, in Peterson's view, an ideal in search of a philosophy, so be it. Ideals have their uses, after all.

NOTES

1. Judith Murrill, *Hutchins Commission*, Freedom of Informa-tion Center Publication No. 69 (University of Missouri School of Journalism), January 1962, p. 1.

2. Robert T. Elson, *The World of Time Inc.* (New York: Atheneum, 1973), p. 79.

3. Fred S. Siebert, Theodore Peterson, and Wilbur Schramm, *Four Theories of the Press* (Urbana: University of Illinois Press, 1956), pp. 78-79.

4. Siebert, Peterson, and Schramn, p. 88.

5. John L. Hulteng, *The Messenger's Motives: Ethical Problems of the News Media* (Englewood Cliffs, N.J.: Prentice-Hall, Inc., 1976), p. 12.

6. Nick Kotz, "The Minority Struggle for a Place in the News-room," *Columbia Journalism Review*, March-April 1979, pp. 26-27.

7. Harold L. Cross, *The People's Right to Know* (New York: Columbia University Press, 1953), p. xiii.

"A Decent Respect"

JEFF GREENFIELD

When I began to think about the issue before us here, I found myself drawn to that famous phrase from the Declaration of Independence: "a decent respect for the opinions of mankind."

It seems to me that this phase contains the essence of what troubles us—or, at least, what troubles me—about the ethical shortcomings of the American press, or "media." It's really not all that useful, after all, to debate the "ethical" questions surrounding the Janet Cooke-*Washington Post* scandal, which bids fair to provide full employment to a generation of media critics, unless the issue of fabricating a press story is considered debatable.

Nor are the other press outrages of recent years—the *New York Times Magazine* account of a Cambodian War actually written from sunny Spain, the *New York Daily News* account of Northern Ireland, wherein participants and quotations were fabricated—ethically complex. Journalists need to worry about how to prevent such incidents, not whether they are right or wrong.

For me, the most troublesome areas have to do with whether we accord "a decent respect" to two very different groups: those we cover as subjects and those we speak to as readers, listeners, or viewers. They are different questions, of course, and yet I suspect that the press's treatment of these two groups and the issue of whether we approach these groups with "a decent respect" are linked to a common flaw of arrogance. And I also suspect that it is this characteristic of the contemporary press that is largely responsible for the

49

less-than-affectionate attitude so many Americans hold in regard to the press.

It may be comforting, somehow, for journalists to tell each other that our difficulties — the spate of libel suits, the anger and resentment at the press — are really political, the effort of a well-heeled group of arch-reactionaries to suppress an aggressive press. The truth, I fear, is different. It is not the press's liberalism or anti-establishment stance that has lost us so many friends. It is, instead, a growing and too often legitimate perception that the media have become themselves a kind of establishment: unaccountable and unwilling to abide by standards of common decency and respect for subject or audience. In this sense, the ethical questions we face are also matters of urgent self-interest.

The first question, then, is what kind of respect we accord to the people we cover. It is surely true that no reporter can drop a newsworthy story because the subject of that story objects; and it is also true that some personal, even intimate secrets of individuals are clearly of public interest.

The drinking problem of a public official is not a "private" matter; nor are the income-tax difficulties of a prominent private citizen; nor, to take a famous case from many years back, is the Jewish parentage of an American Nazi — even if that Nazi threatens to take his own life, if exposed, and carries out that threat.

We are, instead, talking about very different issues: the assumption by the press that once a party enters the public arena, all standards of privacy and taste and — yes, simple decency — go out the window.

Consider some recent examples.

— On national television, Jean Harris is interviewed by Barbara Walters and, through tears and sobs, says yes, she still loves Dr. Hy Tarnower, the man she killed.

— For weeks, the press stakes out the home of Richard Allen, the besieged National Security Advisor, under fire for allegedly accepting gifts. Twenty-four hours a day, cameras and newsmen surround his house; his young child is pursued by the press; cameras grind away each time a curtain is parted.

— As the reign of terror caused by the Atlanta child murders continues, the national and world press hit town. Each child's funeral is covered with saturation attention; on at least one occasion, a cameraman, looking for the best angle of the grieving family, props his camera on the casket of the slain child.

— During that same story, speculation focuses on Wayne Williams. The Atlanta press lay siege to his home, and at least one newsman threatens the father, telling him, in effect, that unless he appears before television cameras, he will be made to look very bad. At the time of this incident, no charges have been filed and no arrest has been made.

— A small-town paper sends an inexperienced reporter to the local courthouse to copy the police blotter. The reporter, misreading the blotter, reports that a well-known local businessman who reported a sex crime was one of those arrested as a sex criminal. The paper argues that it was a "good faith" error and should not be the basis for a libel judgment.

— In Alabama, a camera crew from a local TV station responds to a telephone call from a troubled citizen telling them he will set fire to himself in the town square. The crew calls the police, then videotapes the man as he sets fire to himself; they continue to tape for nearly half a minute before trying to put the fire out.

What these episodes have in common, I think, is that they treat the subject of the story as a means, and nothing but a means, to an end: that end being the production of an emotional interview or photograph or story. And in every case, I think, there is a failure to ask a key question: Given that we have the constitutional right to publish or broadcast this story, should we do it?

That question, I know, would seem fastidious if not ludicrous in many city rooms or TV news headquarters. When a gripping or dramatic story or photo crosses an editor's desk, that editor will usually publish first and ask questions later—if for no other reason than to avoid the embarrassment of losing out to the competition. This judgment is usually explained by invoking "the people's right to know" or an editor's famous comment that whatever God in his wisdom permitted to happen in the world was worthy of publication.

The problem with this defense, of course, is that it proves too much. Every more or less respectable publication has a line beyond which it will not go. The famous NBC film footage of the Tet Offensive, where a South Vietnamese security official summarily executed an enemy agent, was, in fact, edited for reasons of taste. The audience of millions may have been horrified by what it saw at the dinner hour, but what it was spared was the graphic film of blood pouring from the head of the victim. All three television networks aired footage of the death of Karl Wallenda, who fell from a high-wire, but none of them would have aired the videotape of Wallenda's body hitting the ground.

We need not add to the list. The more interesting question is how these limits are arrived at; and why editors and producers do not ask themselves the simple question: "Why am I running this picture or story?" I've talked with enough editors and producers to know the "right" answer to that question: It is to snort, pronounce an elegant obscenity of the kind made famous by Jason Robards in his Ben Bradlee portrayal, and grumble, "Because it's news, dammit!" But, in fact, the occasional public asking of that question would be one of the most profoundly subversive imaginable, because it suggests that the trampling of sensibilities is often, in the most literal sense of the word, indefensible: It is done because the purveyors of news sense that their audience will be intrigued by it, and for no other reason.

Indeed, one of the most amusing aspects of this thinking is to watch what happens when the press itself becomes the victim of this curiosity. Watch the *New York Times* review a new novel, based on the personal eccentricities of the two top editors as well as the matriarch of the owner-family; not a word in the review alludes to these facts. Watch the way television networks bar outsiders from their premises, with security guards and locked doors, and imagine how they would portray a subject's treatment of the press with such protection ("behind these tightly guarded walls, Mr. Dithers refuses . . . ").

There are times, in fact, when the irony of the press's treatment of subjects becomes overwhelming. Last spring, the "CBS Evening News" did a story from the Florida major league spring training camps, focusing on huge salaries being paid some major league baseball players. Here, the correspondent said, is Dave Parker, who is paid $6,000 for every time at bat; here is Dave Winfield, who will be paid $10,000 for every hit. Then the piece ended—and the camera cut to Dan Rather, who is being paid about $8,000 every day he sits down and reads twenty-two minutes of news. He is being paid his salary, of course, for the same reason Dave Winfield is being paid his: He is, in a market sense, worth it. But somehow it did not even occur to CBS to point out that remarkable similarity. That would be considered personally offensive to Dan Rather. Indeed it may be; but then, why treat the ballplayers as if they were somehow different from the reporter?

This is, I think, the first area where the press has to start imposing some ethical constraints upon itself and has to stop assuming that the press is beyond the standards of simple human decency. It comes down to Kant's fundamental ethical principle, which is echoed in sources as diverse as the Sermon on the Mount and Sartre: Treat people as ends, not means, not objects. To ignore the humanity of the subjects of the press, of course, does exactly that: It reduces these people to objects.

But there is a second question about the press which raises the same issue, and that is the way in which the press treats its readers, listeners, and viewers. We used to have a word for these categories: They were our "audience." Now there is a new word: They are our "markets." And the distance between those two words is, in ethical terms, enormous.

Look, for example, at the language of market studies; it is filled with military terms, terms like "targets" and "strategies" and "vulnerabilities." The whole tone of the language is that of war, as if the audience were an adversary that needed to be conquered or tricked into reading or watching.

Or consider some of the favorite weapons in the arsenal of journalism and market research. You gather a focus group, a cross section of citizens, and you ask them to tell you what they want in a local television news show, or a newspaper— and then you give it to them or make them think you are giving it to them. This is defended as "democracy" in action, giving the people what they want; to object to it is, in the favorite phrase of the day, "elitist."

But ask yourself how much respect for the audience this marketing approach really contains. First, it assumes that a reader or viewer cannot be persuaded to pay attention to anything outside of his own immediate interest; it assumes that news must be packaged to appeal to a need for reassurance or diversion or an emotional, compelling, "human" angle that may completely miss the point of the story.

It assumes that the motivations that have drawn people to learn more about the world around them—curiosity, hunger for knowledge, even self-interest—must be defined as narrowly as possible, or else the viewer or listener—the "target" —will be lost.

The "ultimate consumer" of news, under the maketing theory, becomes an object, a means to an end. Of course, every reporter, editor, writer, and producer has always wanted and will always want the biggest possible audience for his wares, but that is very different from turning the news into a packaging device.

Is that happening in the news business? Of course it is; and it has been happening for years. The only questions are how far has it spread and how long will the trend continue? For more than a decade local news stations across the country have turned the local news into a marketing tool; the stories of anchors hired for their piercing blue eyes, wavy blond hair, or musculature are part of the national humor treasury now.

The point, of course, is that in literally dozens of cities, as the salesmen have taken over the local news programs, as this one-time public service has emerged as the key profit center of local stations, the "news" aspect of these programs has been honored more in the breach than in the observance. It is much like the story of the vendor outside the bullfight selling "Hot Meat Pies." A customer bought one and bit into it — and found nothing but cold dough.

"There must be some mistake," the customer complained, pointing to the sign.

"No, señor," the vendor smiled. " 'Hot Meat Pie' — that's the *name* of the pie."

"News" is the name of the show, in many markets.

Or look at network television: that half-hour summary of the day's big events, which network anchors and executives have for years insisted had to be an hour long to have any hope of adequately informing the American people.

In recent months something has been happening on all of these programs. There used to be something called an "end piece" — so called, as you may imagine, because it came at the end of the broadcast. It was usually a light feature — something, for example, about a man who trained snakes to pray or about two relatives who'd been separated at birth and had lived next to each other for fifty years without knowing it.

Now these "end pieces" don't occur at the end any more; they're showing up halfway through the news, or earlier. Why? Because, I think, the people making decisions about these shows seem to be afraid they will lose their viewers if they give them news that is too "complicated" or boring. The "targets" of the news, the theory seems to go, need to be massaged and coddled to stay with the news.

Is this an ethical question? I think it is. Why has the press been given constitutional protection from the kinds of official regulation that is a commonplace in other enterprises? What, after all, is supposed to separate the press from any other business? It is, I think, the idea that the press was to hold a special trust in this free society; it was to be the medium through which people learned about their government, their economy, their country.

But if the press is to be engulfed in a marketing philosophy, if its only purpose is to hold an audience for the next advertiser, then what makes it different from any other purveyor of any other good or service? What makes it better or different from Mobil Oil or U.S. Steel or McDonald's? The answer is: nothing—nothing but the willingness to unsettle, even to unnerve a reader or viewer with something that he had better know.

Here, then, is where the two questions I have tried to raise find their common source: in arrogance. The press seems to think that it can say what it wishes, do what it wishes, invade privacy where it wishes, because it is possessed of a noble mandate. Yet it also seems to think it can act with precisely the same motives as any other business, even if such a marketing philosophy completely negates the "mission" which supposedly justifies its behavior.

I don't believe that kind of doublethink can long endure. I don't believe the public will buy that kind of doublethink; and I don't believe a free press can assert the privileges of a divinely protected priesthood while acting as a carnival barker without undermining its own critically important constitutional freedoms.

This is exactly why these "ethical" problems, far from being some abstract food for academic thought, may turn out to be among those most urgently in need of a solution, if we are to witness the continuation of a genuinely free and aggressive press. Sooner or later, the American people begin to attack powerful institutions that refuse to accept the obligation of accountability. There is no reason to believe that the press can forever be exempt from that historical pattern. The problem, of course, is that if the press becomes such a target, we are all likely to be the loser.

Some Questions That Don't Stay for an Answer

MAX LERNER

I take my title from Francis Bacon's essay "Of Truth." You recall how he started it: " 'What is Truth?' said jesting Pilate; and would not stay for an answer." All prime questions are unanswerable, like Freud's "What is it that women want?" and Wittgenstein's "How get the fly out of the fly bottle?"

I am happy that my friend Elie Abel chose to start by having us revisit Robert Hutchins. He was a formidable presence when I was at Yale. Later he was at once Augustinian and Thomist, believing in the City of Man fashioned in the image of the City of God. His life stretched like a taut rope in a dialogue between the two, and he was a rope-walker over the abyss.

As it happened, 1947 was not only the year of the Hutchins Commission's report, *A Free and Responsible Press*, but the year when Norbert Wiener, that precocious genius, finished writing his *Cybernetics; Or Control and Communication in the Animal and the Machine*, touching on a strange mélange of disciplines—electronic feedback, digital computers, robotry, systems analysis, biophysics, and organismic theory. The late 1940s were thus the seedbed of a good deal that germinated in the traumatic, but also shaping, events of the wild 1960s and 1970s.

1

This leads me to my first question about the Information Era that Wiener ushered in. *How can we translate the ocean*

*of information that floods around us into the understanding
and meaning which are in so short supply?*

We are overwhelmed by the almost unlimited factual access our era opens up, turning the world into a vast archive whose archon the computer has become. But what is important is not the immensity of the expanse but the fact of *selectivity*—we can zero in with lightning speed on exactly what we want. It is the *selectivity* that counts.

This is true also of space research and exploration. We thought it would turn us outward toward untold worlds of space beyond the earth. It has done that. But even more, with the communication satellites, it has turned the earth inward upon itself, recording and transmitting the selective to its target audience, making us all observer-participants of our strange behavior and its consequences. This is what Marshall McLuhan—the third figure in that strange triad of Hutchins, Wiener, and McLuhan—meant when he spoke of the "global village."

There is nothing now that can escape us. We have become the sleuths not only of the cosmos but of our own little earth. There is nothing which leaves a spoor that can evade our unsparing quest. If a sparrow fall the *New York Times*, the *Washington Post*, or "60 Minutes" will be there, and the fall will not go unreported.

My colleague at Notre Dame, John Dunne, has written that once the inevitability of death sinks in on us, we are thrust back on the meaning of life. For many decades we have been involved in the search for the ascertainable facts. We go at them now with a ferocity which raises serious issues about how human beings use other human beings. But say we have achieved the ultimate—to get at everything gettable, even if we do it with a scorched-earth thoroughness. What then?

I suggest that this end-of-the-road achievement shifts the universe of discourse. We come back to what those impenetrable German philosophers called *Verstehen*—not only to know but to understand the *meaning* of what we know. Alas, not all the brilliance of technology or single-mindedness of pursuit eases the thorny path to understanding.

If anything it obscures the path, by persuading us of how much we have achieved by reporting on the fall of the sparrow, perhaps even speeding it with our investigative reporting. I am no doubt biased here. As a true reporter I generally laid an egg. When I "heeled" the *Yale Daily News* in 1920 as a sophomore, I couldn't track down any stories. In 1943, when I asked Ralph Ingersoll—founder and editor of *PM*— for an editorial job, he asked me to bring two specimen pieces. I did. He said, "You'll never be a newspaperman." He was right, within his frame, yet, in a broader sense, I am proud to count myself one. Fortunately he was drafted, and I got the job and found that, even then, there was a hunger for frame and structure and meaning, as there is now. That was the new journalism, even in its excesses.

The meanings don't come ready-made. You have to sweat for them. I came to *PM* from Sarah Lawrence and Harvard and Williams. My newspapermen heroes were William Bolitho and Heywood Broun, but the key figure that linked the academic and journalistic universes together for me was Max Weber. How objective can a historian or sociologist be? he asked. Can his writing be *wertfrei*—value free? The answer was No. Being human, we have values, and we cannot wholly escape them. But we can make a heroic effort to become aware of them, make them explicit, reckon with them, and diminish their distorting impact.

It is still the best answer to the sound and fury of the journalism of the 1960s and 1970s. Yet what detachment we can achieve is only part of the problem. The larger part is to achieve meaning, which can be done only through the frames of experience and questioning we bring to our observation. In that sense journalism is a discipline, like the other *social* or, as I prefer to call them, *human* sciences. It is a very exacting one because, in the absence of training in specialized areas—business, science, technology, defense, literature, the arts, medicine, law—the journalist finds himself forced into being a generalist. Often as not he is unprepared for it. We seem to operate in a vacuum of memory and of context. I can only repeat what Justice Holmes told a class of law students a long time ago: "Your business as thinkers is to see the relation between your particular fact and the whole frame of the universe."

2

My second question follows on the first, since it is about investigative and adversarial reporting. *How do we separate the investigative from the adversarial and both from the potentially destructive?*

A word first about the star reporter. I grew to manhood in the tradition of the great romantic reporters—John Reed, Edgar Snow, Walter Duranty, John Gunther, Vincent Sheehan, Edmond Taylor. They got their drive toward uncovering the hidden from two sources, Marx and Freud. Before them, Lincoln Steffens had stripped city bosses naked to the public gaze. John Reed, who was a Steffens disciple, went to Russia not only to celebrate the revolution but to show up our own lack of one. Lincoln Steffens went, and returned to say, "I have been over into the future—and it works." Warren Beatty followed both Reed and Steffens much later, with *Reds*, but forgot to report what Reed's friends understood—that before his death Reed knew that it didn't work and was heartbroken. Yet as late as the 1930s my friend Harold Laski was still amusing dinner partners with his witticism: "I would rather be buried in the Kremlin with John Reed than in the *Herald-Tribune* with Walter Lippmann."

How did the investigative search become an absolute, and how did the idea of total freedom from restraint come to invest both verbal and non-verbal expression? Elie Abel provides an interesting insight into the movement for the people's "right to know." My own supplementary answer crystallizes around three men—Hugo Black, William Douglas, and Roger Baldwin—because they came to embody some more abstract forces in American intellectual history.

Black marked the harvest of southern Populism and his own sense of guilt about his episode with the Klan; great as he was, he was also a literalist and reductionist in his reading of the constitutional text. Douglas marked the crest of north-western Populism with its sense of the eastern corporate lords as the Adversary. In Baldwin, who founded the American Civil Liberties Union, the American Puritan conscience was magnificently operative. In all three cases, the dissenting tradition was wedded to the strain of perfectionism, guilt, and conceptual polarizing in American religion and thought. It is interesting that a non-Puritan Yankee, Justice Holmes, refused to use the First Amendment as a spear for absolutism and that his disciple, Felix Frankfurter, was even more of a checks-and-balance Madisonian.

Having asked how the search for freedom was invested with the absolute, I ask further how it came to be so adver-sarial in its animus. Behind every search there is a whiff of the satanic to be uncovered. Both Jefferson and Lincoln were hounded by journalists as the anti-Christ. This sort of thing has carried over into the secular era in other forms. The type-figures here are Daniel Ellsberg, in his pursuit of the Penta-gon Papers, and the "Woodstein" tandem of Bob Woodward and Carl Bernstein, in the case of the Watergate cover-up. They remind us again that it takes a great emotional cause, with high political stakes, to act as a propulsive, even a con-vulsive, force in the history of journalism.

In the historical frame one must start with the "Great Promise" and its collapse. I speak of the Kennedy promise and the promise of civil rights, and of the assassination of both Kennedys and of Martin Luther King, which dissipated both promises. In all three assassination cases, the conspiracy hypothesis has never been wholly erased. All three became the focus of intensive amateur searches, to get at the hidden accomplices who disappeared, the unrecovered bullets, the shadowy motivations. It was a kind of manic collective investigative reporting, and it exercised some of the most ingenious minds of our time.

Add the Vietnam war and add Watergate, and you get something like the "Passion of the Republic." The war and Watergate were attended by a marshaling of journalistic talent in an adversary relationship unparalled in American history. They engaged the dreams, ambitions, and self-image of the young and gave journalism a mystique it had never before possessed to an equal degree. The ultimate villain came close to being a wicked government and a sick society. A journalist intensely involved in this adversary relationship was Seymour Hersh, whose *New York Times* exposé of the Intelligence community had a historic impact comparable to Ellsberg's and "Woodstein's."

3

The question which emerges from these — my third question — is a rephrasing of that of Hutchins. *Can we, as a civilization, strike a balance of some sort between freedom and responsibility in the media?* To say "we had better" is not to say that we will. To say it is needed is not to say it will come.

It isn't hard to map the areas where the clashes arise. One is that of the criminal justice system, including the Grand Jury, in which it is difficult to carry out procedures in the face of press publicity or of resistance by the investigative press. I must say that, in the cases of reporters who refused to divulge their sources, I several times found myself envying them in their chance at going to jail for their principles. The need for a survivable martyrdom is deeper within us than we suspect. Besides, it would make a good story.

A second area of clash comes in tracking down corruption, crime, or cover-up, by whatever means may come with the territory, including disguises, lying, and the destructive re-

vealing of secrets. A third, often involved in intelligence
stories, may include putting the lives of secret agents at risk.
A fourth area involves deep intrusions into privacy, in which
the target is not a public official or a person not even perceived as a public figure.

My own feeling is that these are not insoluble problems in
a democracy; the solutions must include a balancing of interests, however, rather than a vesting of any one of them
with absolutism. Neither the British nor the French have
allowed themselves to be caught in the American impasse.
We could do much worse than to move in the direction of the
British Official Secrets Act or their Press Council. For the
present, especially in the area of pornography, we are still
relying on the Supreme Court as final arbiter, using the test
of artistic merit and/or social purpose. But the current Court
flirtation with the idea of using local community standards as
a baseline introduces a mare's nest into what is already
dangerous ground. In other emerging areas of conflict, as
in those involving the morality of gene-splicing or life-
terminating great decisions, for example, the media can be
of great help in bringing the judgments of sensitive physicians, scientists, and theologians to the attention of the nation, thus testing the standards of the involved professions by
the standards of the larger community.

4

My fourth question has to do with *the kind of power the
media exercise and the kind of entity it makes of them.* They
have been called the *imperial media*, and there is a sense in
which the adjective belongs to them even more than to the
presidency. When Louis D. Brandeis, seventy years ago, put
the question to businessmen of whether or not they constituted a profession, he was putting the question of greed to
them—whether this "congeries of possessors and pursuers"

(as Keynes was to call them) could subordinate their bottom-line passion for profits to their self-limiting restraints. With a political governing class, the question has been not one of greed but of power. In the case of the media, it is again one of power, but in a purer and more distilled sense, and the question of self-restraint is thereby the more acute. As Chief Justice Stone put it to his colleagues in *Butler* vs. *U.S.*: "The only restraint we have is our self-restraint."

What is the nature of this power? It is the power over the symbolic structures that govern our thinking and feeling, to whose beat the brain and mind march. It was there all the time, in the form of the printed and spoken word: "In the beginning was the word." Hence the supreme importance of protecting its utterance. But by its very technology, the instantaneous transmission of the word, spoken by living organisms, enacted in the living drama of gesture and tone and relationship, is proving more powerful than the printed word has ever been. By evoking the symbolic structures within which we live and move and have our being, it calls into play what Coleridge knew to be the most powerful human faculty — the *imagination*. *Fortis imiginatio facit casum*, said the Romans: A strong imagination creates the event.

The power of televised images has transformed the impact of war and weaponry. We watch the heaving of the ground in a new nuclear test, and we need to add few words to the argument for a test-ban. We watch the now indelibly imprinted image of the mushroom cloud — as imprinted as with Konrad Lorenz's goslings — and it is hard to think of anything except man's self-destructive drive. We watch the image of the wailing Arab women, in the massacre camps at Beirut, and we need no accompanying words to tell us it is the stuff that makes prime ministers accountable and comes close to toppling governments and — rightly or not — changes the world's assessment of the Israelis.

But when there are so many images available in a cosmos awash with symbolism, it is the *selection* that counts as power. "Ah, but we don't select," the media elite protest, "we only report what is there." To which I say, "Ah, but we do select." And I also say that it is in that power of selection — in news stories encapsulated in sixty seconds or two minutes, in film clips bounced off the satellites circling in space — that power today is wrapped up.

Think of the impact this power has already had on the political process, sharpening everything, bringing the profession of political pollsters and other consultants into being, maximizing the effect of TV political advertising, giving a new importance to private fortunes and political action committees, de-emphasizing sustained political debate after the Lincoln-Douglas model, and putting a premium on the quick take, the devastating statistic, the iterated slogan. It is in this sense that McLuhan was right in saying that it is the medium, with its irresistable impact and its immeasurable plasticity, which is itself the message.

What shall we do with this power? We cannot escape or renounce it, this flaming Nessus-shirt which has become our cultural integument, and which we cannot strip away without stripping away the skin of the culture itself. It is nothing short of a new language that is being shaped, overlapping the verbal language of whose corruptions Edwin Newman has become the chronicler — at once the digital language of mathematics and biophysics and the personal computer and cassette, and the language of powerful symbolic structures that they transmit.

If I understand what the critics of this imperial power are saying (many of them blue-collar, redneck, hard-hat), it is that a new ruling class has come into being. It is not the owning or corporate class but the media elite, unelected, self-chosen (liberal, intellectual, university-based, Establishment), but nonetheless presiding over the destinies of parties, candidates, and presidents and deciding the outcome of the "social" or "cultural" issues which are close to those who live their lives at the level of the culture itself.

How shall we answer them? One man who might have was Herbert Marcuse. He understood the dynamics of co-option, and recommended the "selective intolerance" of "reactionary" ideas which had become his credo. He died, short of the goal of world revolution he had dreamt of, bitter because (as he felt) the "system" co-opts young talent, draining off its revolutionary energies. What we have today is a continuing Left Liberalism, working within the system, largely campus-based, training the best and the brightest in their skills as manipulators of symbolic systems. Marcuse was right: They would rather be stars than Spartacus.

Yet they have the best of both worlds. They become stars, yet retain the edge of Promethean revolt — of stealing fire from the gods on Olympus. It gives life its savor and gives them the validation we all require for sweating away at our work. It enables them — by co-option — to open and close the gates for others and to decide how much circulation of elites there will be.

5

My fifth and final question, necessarily too summary: *How can the psychological effects of the media be mediated, its healthy aspects enhanced, its sick-making aspects diminished?*

I speak, of course, of the mooted question of media violence and its impact on the mind of the child and adolescent, especially in single-parent families living in poverty, where the realities are intolerable and the fantasy life vivid. It will be a long time before we can form any estimate of that carry-over.

But we do already know something about the role of the media in the educational process. The fact is that the media have become the prime educational arena for many, if not most, of our youngsters. They *are* the new public school system, and there is no Horace Mann to organize them for us or guide their influence. If the professional educators don't know what is happening, the classroom teachers and many of the parents do.

It is a question of values formation and values internalizing—functions that the family, the church, and the community have in the past performed. These functions are now performed by a youngster's peer group and the media acting in conjunction, because the media furnish the language, imagery, and symbolism common to the peer group. Much of it is sexual, much is violent, much is criminal. The erotic revolution is being made available to the young of every class, precipitously, if not on radio and the regular television channels, then on cable TV and in cassette form.

One result is what Neil Postman has called "the disappearance of childhood." In the Puritan culture, childhood didn't exist. Children were "little men" and "little women." Yet, if Jean Piaget was right, childhood is built into the stages of innate early cognitive development. Whether invented or rediscovered by our modern age, childhood has become a precious cultural possession, and its loss would be a traumatic one. The internalizing of values, which is the heart of education because it is the heart of character formation, cannot be abandoned to the vagaries of chance media encounters.

* * * * *

We are meeting in the most fluid era of our history, members of the most fluid sector of the society, with the most accelerated rate of change in its technology and impact. If there is some structure of determinism involved, there is also a smell of possibility. Anything can happen—and probably will. There is the stuff of plasticity here. Whatever our ills, immobilism is not one.

There is also the stuff of creativeness here. The same information technology that has presented us with problems presents us also (so the futurists, like Alvin Toffler, Herman

Kahn, and John Naisbitt, tell us) with a creative openness to decentralizing and demassifying, with the hope of achieving a return to the home and family and possibly to religion. Is it impossible to envision the traumatic and the creative walking hand in hand? Remember Nietzsche's vision: "Out of chaos a dancing star."

Journalists: The New Targets, the New Diplomats, the New Intermediary People

GEORGIE ANNE GEYER

When I started at the old *Chicago Daily News* twenty years ago—which we can now use as a neat period to mark the changes in American journalism—ethics could be defined in terms of the "whiskey bottle at Christmas." The work was fairly simple, and so was the conception of ethics.

In work, the reporter needed honesty, accuracy, a good spirit, and (particularly) a grand set of feet. What we did was this: we went out, day after day after day, and conveyed to our readers the announcements of the institutions of our society. It was wholly possible then to be "objective," for the messages we couriers carried were simple and clear. And ethics? Well, ethics was not taking whiskey (or candy, or perfume, if anyone had thought to offer those) at Christmastime. That meant you were "clean."

We loved one another, and we loved newspapering. I may be overromanticizing that period, but frankly I doubt it. There were four papers then in Chicago—imagine, four!— and, while there was ferocious competition *among* the four papers, there was very little among us. The paper at that time was set up so that everyone shared in everyone else's victories. All of this is totally different from today, when reporters within papers are pitted against one another in what has often obnoxiously been called "creative tension."

Life was just so damned much fun—and most of us agreed

that we went into newspapering because there wasn't much else any of us could do. Celebrity? Power? Those words never passed our lips, but we did have a lot of imagination. In the early sixties, for instance, I masqueraded as a waitress to cover a Mafia wedding—and got a wonderful front-page story which led off, "Gangland went to a wedding, and I went along for the ride."

Then, in 1966, when I was a foreign correspondent covering Cuba, I had my first interview with Fidel Castro. Now Castro is a great person to interview—you don't have to ask any questions. He starts talking and about eight hours later he stops. So I was sitting there listening, and suddenly, at 1:30 A.M., he inexplicably stopped. He reached over, woke up the minister of education, who was napping, and said, "José, let's get some ice cream."

Llanusa shook himself, looked at his watch, and said, "No, Fidel, it's too late."

I was totally bewildered but I did guess that they were talking about the elaborate new ice cream parlor across the street. Just then, Fidel looked at me, deadly serious, and said, "We now have twenty-eight flavors."

I was stunned. "Ooh, that's very nice," I answered. That's what I always say when I have absolutely no idea what is going on. (Should I have said, "Do you have strawberry ripple?")

Then he looked at me again and, still dead serious, said, "That's more than Howard Johnson's has."

I was still bewildered, so retorted yet again, "Ooh, that's very nice."

Then Fidel more or less explained—and I thought the answer gave an interesting little insight into his personal obsession with the United States. "Before the Cuban revolution, the Cuban people loved Howard Johnson's ice cream," he said. "And this is our way of showing we can do everything better than the Americans."

When I put this at the end of an otherwise very serious interview with him, the paper the next week sent me a cable in Havana. "Howard Johnson's has responded!" they said. "They now have thirty-two flavors!"

So it went. Until it started to change. And I watched the changes firsthand, first in the Dominican Republic in 1965, then in Vietnam during the late sixties. Suddenly, we journalists were not just conveying the statements of the institutions of society; we were catapulted into a wholly new role. We became what I call, in one of my phrases, the "arbiters of truth."

Now, how did this happen? Well, it happened—and most of us did not in the beginning relish this changed new role—because of Vietnam. There, with so much distrust and dishonesty, we had generals who would take us aside and say, "Look, everything we told you at the briefing today was false. Go out and look at this. . . ." Suddenly it was up to us not just to report but to decide, day after day, what was true and what was false. It was a watershed change in American journalism, and it led to the situation today in which journalists are the new diplomats; in which they are participants in the great play of life and no longer simply the observers in the wings; in which they are the arbiters of truth in an increasingly complex world where there are few absolute truths.

This changeover was not—and is not—without its distinct dangers. Younger journalists soon began talking about ominous things like "telling the truth about society" and about "the search for truth." (I should add that, being from the South Side of Chicago, when someone starts talking about the "search for truth," I reach for my wallet and head toward the door.) Journalism is *not* the "search for truth"—I leave that to the philosophers and the theologians and the poets. Journalism is and must be the search for the little, relative truths that alone keep us sane in the world; *it is the relentless search for what can be known, not for what cannot be known.* And the dangers in trying to make it more than that were shown clearly by the fact that it was a Janet Cooke at the *Washington Post* who chirped, even after her sordid little sortie into self-serving and opportunistic make-believe, that journalism was the "search for truth."

Indeed, by the time a Janet Cooke came, journalism had changed dramatically. Out of the voyage to becoming the "arbiters of truth" came two new forms of journalism: adversary journalism and advocacy journalism. The first supposed a total and unabating hate relationship between the journalist and virtually every institution of our society. (These were the same institutions that only two decades ago we had been so dutifully quoting!) The second supposed that virtually any journalist had the right to put his/her ideas wherever he/she pleased, including in the news columns. Both of these new practitioners were recognizable for their extraordinary self-righteousness. The sweeps of humor that our generation had lived on and lived by did not inform these new Cromwells of the pen.

At the same time, the foreign correspondents—and I was one of these blessed and crazy people from 1964 on—were discovering change "out there" that lent to many of the changes going on at home. First of all, let me say that I believe and know that foreign correspondents have a very special calling. They are more than reporters; they are couriers between cultures, carrying messages from people to people. They are the people who, unlike soldiers or even diplomats, don't have to be there at the ends of the world, but are, for reasons of commitment and curiosity. My book on foreign correspondents, *Buying The Night Flight*, explains the romance and the very special kind of transcendence the work involves; indeed, the title comes from that great aviator and romantic, Antoine de Saint-Exupéry, who wrote, "There is no buying the night flight, with its 100,000 stars, its serenity and its moment of sovereignty."

Well, suddenly it all wasn't so romantic anymore, either. Suddenly we foreign correspondents, along with the diplomats, the businessmen, the Red Cross workers, the missionaries, the priests, and the nuns, became the new targets in a world increasingly disintegrating. In the early years of a Dominican revolution, we had been protected, if only by the aura of American power. Now they wanted *us*. Why?

I began to really see and analyze the changes when I went back to Beirut after the first couple of years of their terrible civil war in 1977. And what I saw was horrifying. It was not war but the absence of war. It was the warning of a world approaching anarchy or what I call "permanent disintegration." All of the rules of non-combatancy, of neutrality, of controls of wars and war situations were no longer observed in this world that had been taken over by what I call the "irregulars": the guerrillas, the commandos, the terrorists, the Khadafys, Khomeinis, and Jim Joneses. It had become what I call "pathological warfare."

When I began nosing around Beirut that spring, I talked, as I always do, with the sociologists and the psychologists, and I discovered that every one of the "armies" that even then were fighting over the once-glorious scraps of that city had become so crazed that they bombed their own neighborhoods, sent artillery into their own people, put bombs in their own theaters. It had become a fighting just to fight and a killing just to kill. It was what the U.S. Army calls "irrational warfare," and it came about when countries began to break down and break apart in the postcolonial period when the Great Powers, for better or for worse, no longer controlled the world.

Now, at the end of each year, I look at the number of countries that have broken down that year, and every year the number grows: Lebanon, Iran, Uganda, Central Africa Republic, Cambodia, Salvador. . . .

Into this same world came leaders far stranger and even more pathological than any we have seen since the Middle Ages. In contrast to the relative innocence of a Castro, now we had men like the Ayatollah Khomeini, who was using the world's most advanced electronic equipment to wage a revolution designed to carry his people back 1,400 years! When I interviewed him in Paris, I was not only amazed at the amount of electronic gear he had around (Satan's Sonys, I called the stuff, since he said that all modern technology was "satanic"), but I was totally disconcerted by the weird way in which he stared between me and my interpreter for over an hour, without ever acknowledging our existence!

Into this new world of the irregulars and of the Khomeinis came the journalists; and soon the journalists became the "new diplomats," for the regular diplomats were either forbidden to talk with these people or were refused audiences with them.

We found the American press, in effect, doing the negotiating with the hostage-holders in Iran, sending messages quite above the heads of the diplomats, directly to the American people. We found a man like Yassir Arafat of the P.L.O. giving his messages intended for the American government to American journalists, who were the only ones permitted to see him. We saw an Anwar Sadat cunningly and cagily learning to use American television as a new form of diplomacy. Sadat felt that the Middle East problem was basically "psychological," so he used his own psychology to reach into the very living rooms and thus the very souls of the American body politic to convince them of it. Now we were different couriers still.

All of these new roles for the journalist have brought on not only great new popularity for journalism and a great new prestige for it but distinct new dangers. Here, in place of the old "whiskey bottle" ethics, are some of the new and far more complicated ethical questions and dangers that I see today:

— The greatest danger today is not the ideological predispositions of reporters, as many believed during the Vietnam war, but rampant careerism.

Let's face it, a lot of the younger journalists have grasped the popular image of journalism in this new age and are in it for the celebrity, the money, and the power. Many of their ethical suppositions leave a lot to be desired. One year, up at the Naval War College at Newport, R.I., Seymour Hersh, the leading investigative reporter for the *New York Times* at that time, gave what is really a perfect example of newspaper careerism.

"National security secrets? That's where it is," he told the officers. "In all my stories, I violate national security. I'm not worried about it. I don't care. I'm a bad news guy. We're entitled to publish any secret we can get and keep. We're such a big country, we can afford it. I publish something and, surprise, the next day the Russians still haven't taken San Francisco." Then, when the officers asked the classical question about the press and national security — "Would you print the story about your country's troopship leaving in times of warfare?" — Hersh said, "Yes, I would. Let it sail another time. Does that make me less of an American?" Then, the really telling line: "Frankly, I'm more worried about the *Washington Post* than national security."

That, my friends, is journalism careerism gone mad.

— Crisis coverage. We are overcovering the crises of the world and undercovering the major trends. Indeed, more and move of the foreign coverage is being done by corps of crises coverers who move from violent conflict to violent conflict — from El Salvador to the Falklands war to the Lebanon war.

This might not at first seem like an ethical dilemma, but it is. The coverage is sensational, not balanced. The coverage does not have as its first concern the telling of important news and the informing of people but the titillation of people. The coverage does not make Americans understand the world better; it causes them to see the world as a very threatening and unnatural place.

This kind of coverage is deeply unethical — and dangerous, too, as most unethical things are. At the same time, there are fewer and fewer serious journalists "out there" really getting the news — the "real journalists" — and more and more here at home, in particular the anchorpeople, who are busily reading and recycling the news and have never been journalists at all.

— Another danger is what I call "dishonesty in style." Janet Cooke was a classic in dishonesty in subject matter, but what about a story that starts out about a high-level business suicide: "He must have felt there was nothing left. He must have felt. . . ." I wondered—did the reporter really go with him? That is dishonesty in style. It is unethical, it is self-serving, it is dangerous.

— The adversariness. We in the press are in considerable danger of removing ourselves from society, like some group of self-righteous monks. And if we remove ourselves from society, as some kind of arbiter or judge, believe me, society will remove itself from us!

Moreover, the very pretense that we can be islands unto ourselves is deeply unethical because we must mix in our society; we must take part in the great dialogue of our people. We, even more than they, need the cleansing and clarifying give-and-take of society. But living with the give-and-take is difficult—it means inner controls in the person involved. And, let us face it, many journalists today do not have inner controls and rational balances—it is oh, so easy, to live beyond the madding crowd and hurl judgments down on it.

And, at the same time, it is all made so much more difficult by the very fact that the importance of the press is so much greater—and so different from what it was. As the great historian James Billington told me one day, "No system survives without some mythological and mythical system. If the need is there and it is not filled by authoritative men and real values, it will be filled by artificial myths and demagoguery. The media has replaced the church. It now provides the value mediators for people's lives. It is the validator of politics. It is where the power is. It is a kind of spiritual power, together with corrosive cynicism."

So, in this new world with all these new roles, where do we go?

— Implicit ethics of the old style must become explicit. We should deliberately and systematically start figuring out what we should do; and we have done this in many areas, as, for instance, in the coverage of terrorist incidents. We should start seriously teaching journalistic ethics.

— We should begin to deal with consequences. We must

see what we are doing to society—and what we are not. We could start by recognizing that we are not a neutral force in a country of limitless security and sanity.

— We ought to begin to understand the world in terms of psycho-political knowledge. I would suggest courses in journalism schools and in newspapers on propaganda, on brainwashing, on the uses of imagery, on the hallucination and the madness of crowds. We must deepen our understanding of the world and of political movements and of political persuasion.

— We should straighten out our thinking. If the "objectivity" of my early years (when it was possible because it was such a simple craft) is no longer possible, let us think about being fair. Let us be sure all sides are given—and fairly. This is not implicit; it is an act of deliberation and will, two qualities which are needed in this new world.

For today, our problems are no longer at the level of the bottle of whiskey at Christmastime or the fifty-dollar handout from the alderman. Today, our problems are deep and abiding and complex; anybody who has covered the Middle East knows just how complex they can be.

I have an idea for a book on journalism ethics that would address this new period. It would be a book of case studies in problem areas, followed by the great philosophical writings from all the great religions and thinkers that apply. . . . This is the kind of universalism we need today.

The Executive Branch and the Fourth Branch

ROBERT J. McCLOSKEY

In agreeing to consider this topic, I was asked to address the ethics of both the executive branch and the fourth branch. I took that to mean the breaches thereof; the kind that occur between and within these two estates. I thought immediately of Oscar Wilde; in giving voice to "the unspeakable pursuing the uneatable," he had in mind less the fox hunt than the coming nature of government/press relations.

A year ago I closed the book on twenty-six years in the Foreign Service, ten of which I spent as press spokesman for the Department of State. The next day I set up business as an independent news critic ("ombudsman" is the trade's preferred designation) at the *Washington Post*. That's the place that's now almost as big as the foreign policy agency was when I entered it.

It wasn't long before the newspaper and the State Department were in an ethical flap. A still-unnamed department official handed a *Post* reporter a summary of his notes from staff meetings of the then Secretary of State Alexander Haig. The paper had been running down rumors that Haig was close to a nervous breakdown. The notes were presumed to document that Haig was on top of things and, indeed, making sense of them. Among other subjects, he was quoted as referring to the British foreign secretary of the day as "a duplicitous bastard."

The *Post* published a front-page story, including the above quote. Immediately critics from inside the government (some from outside) jumped on the paper for its breach of ethics. In a column, I jumped on the unnamed official, holding that no newspaper would refrain from publishing this material and that the question of ethics was misaddressed. I didn't feel the story warranted front-page treatment, however, because not all of it was newsworthy. The piece did Haig more good than harm.

You remember l'affaire de David Stockman, and the *Atlantic Monthly* and the *Washington Post*. William Greider, who wrote the *Atlantic* piece and has since left the *Post*, where he was assistant managing editor for national news, has written an interesting account of the ground rules he felt were operating as he talked with Stockman over several months. Greider saw them one way; Stockman another.

The questions: What about an editor writing for an outside publication on topics he is responsible for at the newspaper? How is the interest of the paper's subscribers protected? (*Post* readers were never given the text of the *Atlantic* article.)

There are other cases in point.

— In midsummer, one of those "over-the-transom" notes landed on my desk. Unsigned, as this type always is, it was on the stationery of my alma mater, the State Department. It was addressed to the *Post*'s publisher, with a copy to me. It made a charge that the paper had doubtless been infiltrated by a Soviet agent. This raving deduction was reached on the basis of two Sunday columns the paper had run on Yuri Andropov, who had just succeeded Leonid Brezhnev. Subsequently, the State Department officially disowned this gaucherie. It can only be hoped that rational heads there will squelch the unethical ones.

— Whether national security adviser Richard Allen deserved to lose his job may be argued. What, it seems to me, can't be condoned is the way the man and his family were hounded by the media, particularly the electronic media. I felt that the way they were treated was, well, unspeakable and begged for some examination of basic ethics in the profession. To date I've read one critical commentary which had about as much effect as a stone dropped into a pond.

Aside from a greater need for policing within, how do these two branches — infinitely adversarial — view one another?

There is a tendency in government to assume that the only right story is the one that properly reflects its view and that recording criticism or conflict is the result of mischievous intent. Simultaneously, the journalist wants more every day than the government is capable of delivering and, more seriously, is less prepared to take the government at its word than ever before.

Collectively, government is intimidated by the press. Its basest inclination is to wish the press would go away and not interrupt the geniuses at work. In the diplomatic profession there remains a fair remnant of an early notion that the requirements of negotiation and those of public information are always locked in almost total conflict. Even those who don't believe this, believe the government was given the short end of the stick, that Thomas Jefferson was talking through his hat in saying, "If I had to choose between a government without newspapers . . ." and the rest of it.

The press looks across at an institution wanting to declare everything secret except where it's self-serving; unless the official is pressed hard, nothing would be forthcoming; that it is wiser to trust the Congress than the executive branch; that if it didn't push or prod (threaten?), the public would go uninformed or, worse, deceived. And there's some evidence for this.

In the daily Washington interplay, I submit, neither of these estates has a corner on morality. I have known dishonest officials and dishonest journalists. Let me restate that: officials and journalists who, on occasion, behaved dishonestly. At worst, I suppose, they're cheaters; cheating with what was said and what was reported. It's no defense, however, to acknowledge there's a little larceny in all of us. What is required is that both institutions work continually and hard to maintain the integrity and credibility with the citizenry.

On the subject of the "daily rounds": Beyond official briefings (noon at the White House and State Department), a tangled web of journalist/public official contacts form the relationship in Washington. Fourth estate working stiffs meet with official working stiffs in offices, at lunch, maybe at neighborhood P.T.A. meetings. At another level bureau chiefs, editors, columnists—the estate's House of Lords—may entertain assistant secretaries at fancy dinners. All this is often referred to as submerged communication.

Less numerous, though not less negligible, are contacts journalists establish with foreign diplomats. I recall being told once by a reporter that the State Department should take pains to point out to the Russians when a particular story in the press was wrong. The reporter, who lunched regularly with a member of the Soviet Embassy, said there were certain columnists and reporters whose articles the Soviets took as gospel on the view of our government. What made this disturbing was that one of the writers mentioned was often far from accurate in describing U.S. policy.

In the movie *Dr. Strangelove*, if you will recall, the Soviet ambassador announces that his country has built a doomsday device, rigged to destroy the earth, after learning the U.S. was going to construct one. Where had the Soviets gotten that idea? In heavy accent, the ambassador replies: "We read it in the *New York Times*."

On the subject of lies: The record of this worst of sins can leave neither institution comfortable. I know of no deliberate decisions to do so at the executive level in the press. I know of a horrendous one made at the highest level of government — the U-2 espionage plane. My State Department spokesman predecessor was lied to by his bosses and, in turn, was maliciously made a public liar.

I lied once unknowingly, after being assured the issue in question had not occurred. It concerned a five-year-old incident about which only John Kennedy, who was then dead, and former Secretary of State Dean Rusk, who was away from Washington that day, knew. Dean Rusk and I both corrected the record and apologized to the press the next day.

Washington Post editors, as you know, were lied to, and the newspaper was made a public liar in the Janet Cooke case. A libel suit will soon be decided between CBS and General William Westmoreland over a network program alleging that U.S. military officials were lying to one another in Vietnam and, in turn, to their civilian leaders. The *New York Times* unwittingly lied to its readers not long ago, when a long article in its Sunday magazine proved to have been faked. The *New York Daily News* fired a reporter for faking stories from Northern Ireland.

Perhaps the most insidious form of deception occurring in newspapers is plagiarism — what Roy Peter Clark has referred to as "kidnapping words." I have already devoted three columns to astonishingly blatant cases, in one of which *Washington Post* material was plagiarized. The tendency to crib under pressure of deadlines is understandable; there's no excuse, however, for failing to credit another's work.

On the subject of looking inward: I'm aware of some of the self-examination underway in journalism. It was pretty provocative for Kurt Luedtke, former executive editor of the *Detroit Free Press*, to tell America's publishers last spring: "There's no such thing as the public's right to know. You made that up, taking care not to specify what it was that the public had a right to know. The public knows whatever you choose to tell it, no more, no less. If the public did have a right to know, it would then have something to say about what it is you choose to call news." Earlier in his remarks, Luedtke, who wrote *Absence of Malice*, noted: "Many people who have dealt with you wish that they had not. You are capricious and unpredictable, you are fearsome and you are feared because there is never any way to know whether this time you will be fair and accurate or whether you will not. And there is virtually nothing that we can do about it."

Barely had this been said when Mike O'Neill, at the time still editor of the *New York Daily News*, was telling America's editors that the fourth branch's "tendency has been to revel in the power and wield it freely, rather than to accept any corresponding increase in responsibility." Noting official deceits and masquerades, he observed, "No longer do we look on government only with the healthy skepticism required . . . we treat government as the enemy . . . and government officials as convenient targets for attack and destroy missions. . . . Have we become so cynical, so hardened by our experiences with sham, that we can no longer feel what an official feels, what his wife and children feel, when he is being ripped and torn on TV and in the press?"

This is potent stuff, which, to date, has had only partial release and, as near as I can tell, no evident effect on the way newspapers are going about their daily business. In fairness, though, I should note that, in a subsequent journalism seminar, *Post* executive editor Ben Bradlee registered disagreement with O'Neill. "Mike talks about the press's harshly adversarial posture towards government. Baloney. I think the press . . . is so g.d. scared now of its new image as all-powerful that we are being too timid. I suggest that the press has been easier on Reagan than on any president in my memory. . . . " Ben knows that I disagree with him. I have said so in a column in the *Post*.

I'm unable to say how much discussion on parallel lines goes on in government—whether officials have undertaken a performance appraisal. The Reagan administration, we know, has hunkered down behind some drawbridges which give reporters difficulty. I'm distressed about this. It's one thing to want to organize and coordinate information and news policy to aid government to speak with a coherent voice, if that, in fact, is the intention. Reporters are saying their access to officials with the right dope has been restricted.

I want to see a more mature, less mistrustful approach toward one another. It seems strange to be saying that this late in the game.

> Whether we're talking about foreign relations or domestic affairs, government will be judged for its actions in the space the press reserves for commentary. It has the right, though, to expect the fairest possible coverage in the news columns. And, it shouldn't confuse the two. Neither should the press.
>
> It never ceases to surprise me how very often in situations of only more than ordinary pressure the two operate in fundamental ignorance of one another. What both sides condemn as unfair . . . can be attributed to continuing ignorance and suspicion. . . ."

I said that ten years ago in a speech to the National Press Club. Regrettably, it is still worth repeating. Society should not feel it must choose one as more credible than the other. The public interest cannot be equated with that of the government alone, nor of the press—and certainly not because one side is shouting at the other: "Your end of the boat is sinking."

The Ethics and Economics of Journalism

LEONARD SILK

I start with a simple and obvious proposition: "In our country, journalism is a business." Hence we cannot look only at the relations between journalism and other business organizations but must consider journalism as a special kind of business. There are some nonprofit journalistic institutions in this country, but the bulk of our newspapers, magazines, television and radio networks and stations are profit-making enterprises.

My second proposition is this: "But journalism is more than a business." Is that a truism? Is it not also true of Standard Oil of Indiana or any other business? My answer is yes, but not really—or not in the same degree. In the case of a newspaper (forgive me if I use the term "newspaper" as a metonymy for all the news media), the aim is not just making money but is also essentially the same as the business of a university: truth-seeking, truth-telling.

We are not the only business heavily freighted with the public interest. Take the medical profession. It, too, is a profit-making industry, if you like, and it has done very well, thank you. At the same time, no doctor worthy of respect would or should behave in a way that is purely profit-maximizing. We have had strong statements, especially from some academic economists, that maximizing profit is and should be the only goal of a business; Professor Milton Friedman has contended that any other goal is subversive of free enterprise and democracy. Without accepting that extreme statement, I do regard profit-making as the prime goal of any business, a necessity for its survival.

That holds for newspapers, too. And the necessity of making money inevitably creates tensions within the press. Can a newspaper simultaneously be both a business serving its own interest and affect to be a quasi-public institution serving everybody's best interests, as defined by the newspaper itself? That question, in my view, creates most of our problems, internally as well as externally. Yet that second function, serving the public interest, which is sometimes forgotten, denied or decried by our critics, including business critics, is a mission to which the public, including business, wishes to hold us. Time and again I have heard business critics of the press say, "What do you guys think you are doing? You're just trying to sell newspapers." That criticism implies that we should not be trying to sell papers, to make money.

If I wanted to be nasty and dishonest, I would reply, "So what are you doing? Just selling pharmaceuticals? Just selling oil? What's the matter with that?" More honestly, I would say: "You're right. The business of a decent newspaper is not just to sell papers and make money." I don't think anybody in his right mind believes that a great newspaper's purpose is just to make money or that its greatness is defined by how much money it makes.

How can the press discharge its public responsibilities better? If there were more time and space, I might wax philosophical about the need to have the media, like other key institutions, such as the university and the church, free of the need to peddle themselves to raise money. They cannot freely pursue the truth if they have to hawk their wares day by day, running the danger of pandering to the marketplace. Incidentally, you can find this doctrine set forth in an eighteenth-century tome, *The Principles of Moral and Political Philosophy*, by the Rev. William Paley. A great university, like Notre Dame, has some breathing room, and no one who ob-

jects to, say, what Father Ted Hesburgh has to say about a
nuclear freeze can hurt Notre Dame. That is a magnificent
thing. Some advertisers may feel that they can hurt the *New
York Times* by pulling out their advertising, and sometimes
they may hurt it a bit, at least temporarily, but they have not
caused it to swerve from its course.

The *Times* is large and strong and hard to hurt. But that
may not be true of many other papers, especially small-town
ones. It takes a lot of guts on the part of the local publisher
to put his paper on the line when the local advertisers come
down on him over some story. I think that the television
networks ought to be braver than they are and less profit-
oriented than they are, but that is another story. They probably could afford to do it, but I think they are more suscep-
tible to pressures than we are, if I may so pride ourselves.

What are the alternatives to our kind of commercial journalism? One is obviously a government-sponsored (and hence
controlled) press, but I think it not unfair to compare *Pravda*,
Izvestia, and other government papers to our own newspapers. A United Nations organ has compared them, I must
say, and found the Communist papers superior to our own.
I think this is nonsense, and I doubt that any American
would want to debate me seriously on whether it would be
better if the government were the source of all news, the con-
troller of all news, as in Communist and other totalitarian
countries. This is no abstract matter. The American press was
commended by Father Hesburgh during this conference for
the role it played in the 1960s, in covering and analyzing the
Vietnam war and the civil rights movement, and in the early
1970s, for the work done on the Pentagon Papers and Watergate. I am grateful for his view. These were crucial, thrilling
demonstrations of the vital role of the press in making this
a better and freer society. Did the press perform its role per-
fectly? Certainly not. These are human institutions, which,
therefore, make mistakes.

Times change. New sins are committed. Public moods
change. But I really do feel that that stretch of a decade or

a decade and a half was, on the whole, a heroic vindication of what Jefferson said about a free press. Everybody, even a president or founder of a nation, is entitled to a crack once in a while. But Jefferson's joke about preferring newspapers over government, if he had to choose, was vindicated in the late 1960s and early 1970s. And remember that it was a commercial press that waged the good fight.

The only alternative I seriously see to a commercial press is one sponsored and financed by foundations and other charitable institutions. But, depending on the sources of the financing and the rigidity of the controls, that might give us a worse press than we have. Why worse? Because it would be tamer, less vigorous, less well-financed — it takes a lot more money than even Father Hesburgh can raise to pay for the *New York Times*. I mean $700 million or $800 million a year for one newspaper. You might say, of course, that America would be better off with a less well-financed press, but I don't think so. We need better and more foreign coverage, to start with, than we are getting. And we need more specialists in major areas of the news, such as economics, science, medicine, and military affairs. We cannot match most faculties in the quality and depth of resources in a number of critical areas, and we ought to do so, given the responsibilities we carry.

That situation is changing dramatically, and I think that we at the *Times* have done relatively well; we do have specialists in law, medicine, economics, military affairs, science, and other crucial fields. That is not to say that every journalist ought to be a specialist; we will need wonderful, enthusiastic, dedicated reporters whom we can turn to on any story, and we are still getting them. In brief, we need both specialists and generalists.

I believe we know that we need to have a better commercial press. The first and most important principle is the separation of the business side from the news and editorial staffs. In a book I wrote with my son Mark, *The American Establishment*, the chapter on the *New York Times* is titled, "Church,

State and Counting House." Everybody talks about the separation of church and state, and, at the *Times*, church refers to the editorial page and state to the news department. In our book we referred to the business side as the counting house, although the business people seem to have got it into their heads that they are the state and the news and editorial departments are the church. In any case, the separation of these functions has always been strongly enforced at the *Times*. I will not say that no sin against that principle has ever been committed, but it is very rare. You cannot make human beings perfect, but you can post guidelines, ethical rules, and that we do.

The second principle that should protect journalists and make the press a better institution is professionalism. While maintaining high professional standards ought certainly to be a major responsibility of publishers and top editors, I think it is up to reporters and other editors to insist on such standards and carry them out voluntarily and determinedly. You can't get something for nothing. If you are going to be a tough and honest reporter and a good person, you have to be prepared to pay the price and not necessarily to expect a reward. You do the job for its own sake, because it is the right thing to do. Ultimately, that protects you and your paper, whether it is immediately appreciated or not. Your paper may wind up grateful, or it may wind up sacking you, but it should not make a damned bit of difference. Now that is big, brave talk, coming from someone who is close to the end of his career and has enough money in the bank. But I understand full well what the problems are. And they are like the problems in every other walk of life — in business organizations, in politics and government, in religion and everywhere else. It is a question of conscience and service in a cause which you deem to be worthy.

I call it professionalism, but it goes beyond professionalism. It is knowing and having the guts to tell what you know. I agree with what Georgie Anne Geyer believes — that the enemy of truth-telling is careerism.

How can we make sure that people do not subordinate their conscience to their careers? And how can we protect those who do their jobs well—but possibly in ways of which their bosses disapprove? There is no easy answer. Since most people, by definition, are average and are not heroes or martyrs, how they behave depends partly on the leadership they get, partly on the standards and courage of their colleagues, partly on the institutional safeguards to their jobs. I am old-fashioned enough to think that, with all its faults, the American Newspaper Guild is still an important institution. You have to go through a lot of trouble to fire a reporter nowadays without just cause. A reporter may still suffer in some way; he may be chained to a copy desk or passed over for promotions or assignments he should have had. But the old-style summary dismissal for any insubordination or some trivial offense is largely gone; and I feel that, in that sense, Heywood Broun, founder of the Guild, did God's work, and it remains to be carried forward.

What other safeguards do we need against bad performance by the press? I think ombudsmen are a good thing. We don't happen to have one at the *Times*, and I think we could use four or five of them. I think the News Council approach is a somewhat weak reed to lean on, because a council can look at only so many things at a time. I confess that I am a little concerned about its becoming a censor, but, on the whole, I am in favor of it as a group of press professionals who are disinterested and can offer intelligent and experienced criticism of the press.

I think the strength of our country, and of our news media, has been its diversity, and I want papers and individuals who will say what they mean or believe, even if other people think they are outrageously wrong.

I don't like our country to get too tidy or uniform. I am worried about the trend toward monopoly in the press. Over 90 percent of our towns and cities have only one newspaper. What frightens me is the possibility that a day will come when there will be a no-newspaper town that gets along, or

thinks it does. I am afraid of a growing illiterate public th
forgets that it needs what a free, courageous and competiti
press can do. I believe it is crucial that all groups, wheth
they are blacks, Hispanics, whites, Catholics, Jews, or wha
ever, have adequate access to a truly free and representativ
press.

Finally, on the issue of the news media versus business,
don't think things are as bad as they have been. We have ha
enough dialogue now for the past ten years between the pres
and business to have built up greater understanding. Botl
institutions have to recognize the differences between then
and the legitimacy of both. There probably are some youn$
reporters who think that oil companies are inherently evil, ex
cept when they want to drive into a filling station and say
"Fill it up." And there are probably some reporters who think
the whole business system is rotten and corrupt. But the overwhelming majority are sophisticated enough to ask the question, "Compared to what?" Compared to the Soviet Union?
To Poland? To El Salvador? To Chile?

That is not to say that I think our system cannot be improved or that every business is ethically run. But I feel that,
after a time, one does wake up to the realization that other
institutions, including businesses, have a right to do their job
and that there is an overall system which is coherent and
which can operate under law quite freely, with many serious and reasonably conscientious human beings in charge of
them.

So whose side am I on, that of business or the press? Both.
But there are differences between them in perspective and
mission. Businesses do love to make money and to see the
value of their stock go up; so do newspapers. But one important difference is that publishers can't control their staffs, at
least not what they see and think and write. A wise publisher
will always say to a complaining businessman, "I'm sorry, but
I cannot control these people." And if he can, it's not a good
newspaper.

Responsibility in Journalism:
A Business Perspective

JOHN E. SWEARINGEN

Let me say at the outset that I find in this occasion a rather daunting challenge. Our subject is journalism, which might be defined as the art and science of using words. And, during this conference, we are listening to some of the finest scientists and artists in the field. Therefore, as a businessman whose area of experience lies in a totally different direction, I feel somewhat out of sync — perhaps the way Dan Rather or Edwin Newman would feel if they were asked to lecture to a group of oil company executives on the most efficient ways to find and produce crude oil and natural gas.

Nevertheless, despite the disparities in purpose and function, business and journalism — for better or worse — are locked together in a symbiotic relationship. And the power of the press in that relationship can be awesome. Kurt Luedtke, former executive editor of the *Detroit Free Press* and author of *Absence of Malice*, recently told a gathering of newspeople: "On your discretionary judgments hang reputations and careers, jail sentences and stock prices, Broadway shows and water rates. You are the mechanism of reward and punishment, the arbiter of right and wrong, the roving eye of daily judgment. You no longer shape public opinion, you have supplanted it."

Those are strong words indeed, perhaps a bit stronger than the facts merit. For my own part, I am not prepared to agree totally that the press has "supplanted" public opinion. However, I can say from firsthand experience that the ability of the news business — and it is a business — to shape public opinion is formidable. When the cause is just and the newspeople who cover it and comment on it possess and assess the facts and issues, then the news business is undoubtedly a force for good. There is no greater safeguard for the survival of our democratic institutions and our way of life than an informed and aroused public.

However, when that same public is aroused, but misinformed, the opportunities for mischief are endless. And here again, I would like to quote from Luedtke's remarks:

> There are good men and women who will not stand for office, concerned that you will find their flaws or invent them. Many people who have dealt with you wish they had not. You are capricious and unpredictable, you are fearsome and you are feared, because there is never any way to know whether this time you will be fair and accurate or whether you will not. And there is virtually nothing we can do about it.

Again, those are strong words, and I do not endorse all the sentiments which inspire them. In the case of this last statement, for instance, I would argue that in many cases, there is indeed something we can do about it. For one thing, if we choose, we can go to court, as William P. Tavoulareas, the president of Mobil Corporation, recently did. He believed that a series of articles in the *Washington Post* concerning activities involving him and his son were not only false but were published with reckless disregard for their truth or accuracy.

As you know, the jury agreed, finding for Bill Tavoulareas. And I find the reaction of the press — whether or not the verdict is successfully appealed — to that finding to be most informative. For instance, the executive editor of the *Wall Street Journal* had this to say: "It's a great commentary on our times when a jury finds for an oil company against a newspaper."

Now I find that statement somewhat astonishing. Indeed, if I might paraphrase, I could observe that it is a great commentary on our times when the executive editor of what is thought of by many as a pro-business newspaper can publicly display what strikes me as a deeply held but no doubt unconscious anti-business bias. Or perhaps it's simply an anti-oil company bias.

At any rate, whatever the psychological roots of that bias, the *Wall Street Journal*, like all successful newspapers, is itself a business, its primary purpose being to sell words and ideas. And it is as a consumer of words and ideas—just as you are all consumers of oil and gas—that I offer my observations.

As a consumer of news, I am as bemused and concerned as any of my fellow citizens by trends in contemporary journalism—trends exemplified by instances such as the Tavoulareas case, the suit brought by General Westmoreland against CBS, the *Penthouse* and *National Enquirer* cases, and the fabricated article in the *New York Times Magazine* about a reporter's trip to Cambodia. As we all know now, he never left home. And of course I would be remiss if I did not mention the Pulitzer Prize-winning *Washington Post* reporter whose story was also totally fabricated.

However, my purpose here is not to excoriate the media—even though, as a member of the oil business, I believe my industry has taken more than its share of lumps in recent years, just as the media are increasingly taking their lumps today. As an oil man, I may feel somewhat paranoid. But in real life, even paranoids have enemies.

If I may, let me—as an oil man and a consumer of news—attempt to tell you why I feel this way. Throughout much of the past decade, especially during the period following the Arab oil embargo of 1973-74 and subsequently during the Carter administration, it seemed to those of us who work in the oil industry that we were routinely accused of every transgression to which mankind falls prey.

Perhaps some of you remember those stories with which we were all bombarded. There was a shadowy conspiracy between the oil companies and OPEC, we were told. In some cases, it was asserted, we were either hiding the products we produce or purposely capping wells in order to drive up prices. In other cases, we were accused of withholding products by slowing down transportation—and some now discredited sources claimed to see fully loaded tankers lurking off the shores of various parts of the country waiting for prices to rise.

Then, just to put the icing on the cake, we could expect an almost daily barrage of invective by those politicians and special interest spokesmen who enjoyed automatic access to the media, especially the electronic media. We were "rip-off artists" and "profiteers," we were told. Our profits were characterized as "obscene," "sinful," and even "pornographic." To put it mildly, this was a bit hard on our morale.

Having said that, however, let me add that I do not mean this as a blanket indictment of the media. If, for instance, the president of the United States chooses to make strong and unflattering statements about an industry, that is obviously news.

However, as valid as that observation may be, it does raise serious questions about the nature of the news. Walter Cronkite once put it this way: "A cat in the alley is not news, but a cat in the tree is." However, if all you focus on and talk about is the cat in the tree, then the public which consumes your stories will eventually come to think that that's the norm.

Sensationalism, in other words, is perhaps the single most important element in shaping the news—and this is especially true of television news. And sensationalism, by definition, must inevitably give rise to distortion.

During recent years there has been a good deal of discussion about these topics, often centering on the subject of bias. That is a subject I won't attempt to address, although I must admit to a certain sympathy with Irving Kristol, who made the following observation in the *Wall Street Journal*. As Kristol put it, the media are permeated with a "liberal bias." In Kristol's opinion: "That bias is self-evident. In truth, it is so deeply ingrained by now that the people at the television networks and on the national news magazines are sincerely convinced that a liberal bias is proof of journalistic integrity."

Depending on your bias—or your lack of bias—you may agree or disagree with that assertion. However, Kristol then goes on to make a point which I believe cannot be argued. He observes: ". . . in all fairness, one must quickly add that there is at least as much sheer mindlessness at work here as there is bias. The media—and television especially—is most influential during moments of panic and crisis, when people turn to it for instant information. It is therefore as natural for the media to lean toward panic-mongering and crisis-mongering as it is for a plant to lean toward the sunlight."

You may find "mindlessness" a rather strong term, perhaps even more offensive than "bias" or "distortion." But in my opinion, there is a pattern here, repeated time and time again, and especially with the electronic media. Whether we like it or not, there is no other medium in the nation which approaches the reach and impact of television.

Surveys are inexact on the subject, and at least one recent study raises certain doubts. Nevertheless, I believe it accurate to say that the vast majority of the American people depend primarily upon television for their information on public affairs and national issues. Therefore, if television offers them a steady stream of biased, distorted, sensational, or mindless information and if that happens on a regular basis, then the aroused public I spoke of earlier will invariably translate those emotions and that misinformation into political terms, and that means the formulation of bad—and perhaps even dangerous—public policy.

Let me give you an example of what I mean here, drawn from my own area, the oil industry. And before I do so, let me identify my own special bias—if you haven't already guessed. To put it briefly, I am an unabashed believer in private enterprise and the market system.

If that is anachronistic, so be it. In my opinion, an irrefutable case could be made to demonstrate that our private-enterprise economic system is the finest and most beneficial means of ordering human affairs yet devised by the mind of man. But I am not writing here as an economic or political philosopher. Instead, for our purposes, suffice it to say that I believe many journalists are either uninformed about or are dismissive of the principles which animate our economic system. And I believe this to be especially true of television journalists.

I think here particularly of the coverage of two periods of serious oil shortages — 1973-74 and 1978-79. At the outset, I think it safe to say that the coverage was, at best, uneven. After the initial shock, however, numerous newspapers and magazines came to grips with the situation and did thoughtful and serious analyses of what came to be called "the energy crisis."

This was not so with television. Nor is this just my own opinion. The Media Institute, a nonprofit research organization funded by 300 corporations and foundations — among them the American Broadcasting Company and Warner Communications — has undertaken an extensive study of television coverage of those so-called crises. And the conclusion is that Americans received a steady stream of misinformation from each of the three major television networks.

Space does not permit me to share the study's findings with you in detail, but perhaps a sampling will suffice. In a series of evaluations based on analysis of some 1,462 oil-shortage stories during the period, the study found:

— Non-market solutions, such as conservation, rationing, regulation, and price controls, received three times more coverage than did market solutions (63 percent to 21 percent).

— Only 15 percent of the solutions aired dealt with the major policy issue of regulation and price controls versus deregulation and decontrol.

— Prices were depicted as a problem rather than a possible solution.

— The largest single source of information was the government. The networks used government spokesmen to discuss solutions 77 percent of the time; oil industry sources, 9 percent of the time.

— Government was identified as a possible cause of the shortages 18 percent of the time; OPEC and the oil industry, 72 percent of the time.

— When causes were being discussed, the oil industry was accused of perpetrating a hoax, profiteering, withholding supplies, or other devious actions 25 percent of the time.

From these and numerous other particulars, the study draws the following conclusion: "The networks paid scant attention . . . to the general political and economic policy at stake: non-market solutions versus market solutions. Rather, the networks generally presented the solutions to the oil crises as a choice of non-market measures: conservation versus rationing versus forms of regulation and price control."

Was that coverage the result of bias? Or was it simply sensationalism, growing out of the basic mindlessness of the medium? I will not attempt to answer those questions. However, I would like to make a few personal observations. The problem, in my opinion, lies with the nature of the beast.

Television imparts information in several ways. There are the news programs themselves, usually little more than brief rewrites of wire copy or today's front page, with talking heads or sensational camera footage thrown in—hardly the format to deal with complex economic issues.

Then there are the talk shows, upon which from time to time I force myself to appear. Such appearances are not one of life's great pleasures, and usually the best I can hope for are non-hostile and semi-intelligent and informed interlocutors. But I long ago decided I could not abandon the stage to our detractors. If we would not speak up for ourselves, then whom could we expect to do so?

Finally, there are the occasional specials, where an extended interview with a network crew can be edited down to a few seconds of comments, often tailored to make the interviewee look and sound as villainous as possible.

I have had several rather distasteful experiences in this regard. But one that stands out sharply in my mind occurred during 1978. In that year, a television crew from one of the major networks proposed to do a feature story on the complex problem of natural gas price regulation—an economic problem, incidentally, which continues to plague us today. Suffice it to say that the proposed story was to be aired on one of those "in depth" programs, which purport to get behind the headlines and down to bedrock basics.

Now, the natural gas pricing situation was, and still is, as complex as Medusa's hairdo, and just about as attractive to deal with. But the way in which the television crew approached that nest of snakes is quite instructive.

First, they bounced around the state of Texas, talking to some of the most unrepresentative people they could find. Then they came to Chicago, where I gave them an interview. That interview lasted for about an hour and forty minutes. And, early on, two things became apparent to me: the interviewer had no more knowledge of the natural gas situation than I have of needlepoint; and she was working from a prepared script, hoping to goad me into giving her a few outrageous answers that would fit into that script. The show, in other words, was already in the can.

I tried, as patiently as I could, to discuss the basic economics of the situation with her. But that was not what she wanted. What she wanted, instead, was some on-camera proof that big oil was out to rip off the consumer. I didn't oblige, and in the subsequent show, as aired, I found that they used less than one minute of that one hour and forty-minute interview.

But my own role is unimportant here. What *is* important is that the show, the ostensible purpose of which was to explore economic facts in depth, was, in reality, a sensational attack upon my industry and upon compromise legislation then pending in Congress.

In short, that particular show epitomizes all the elements I have mentioned. It was mindless, since it reflected no understanding of the situation. It was inaccurate, with its basic contentions framed within a set of skimpy and easily discredited statistics. It was dishonest, built on numerous errors in fact and deceptive and selective editing. And, in a very basic sense, it was totally biased.

I don't use the word *biased* here primarily in an ideological or political sense, although the case certainly could be made. Rather, I refer to the nature of the medium itself. Television is indeed biased, but its bias lies in the direction of the immediate, the easily understood, the sensational, the emotional. You can, if you like, call it news. But actually, it's really just show business.

What is required for television is the quick, easy answer, the scene that stirs people up, the emotional hook which will cause the ratings to jump. And, I suppose, from the point of view of the television producer, there could be nothing more deadly in the vicious ratings game than a long discussion of the facts and figures of an extremely complicated economic program.

It is far preferable, from a show-business point of view, to reduce it all to easy, emotional terms. And so, after scouring the state of Texas, the network crew finally found an appropriate family in Austin, willing to talk about the size of their gas bills. And the anchorperson boiled the whole enormous economic problem down to this: Eventually, she said, if our industry had its way, people might "one day have to choose between air conditioning their homes or sending their children to college."

But enough. I am not writing here to chastise television newspeople, or any other newspeople, for that matter. If that were my intent, I might point to those problems that businessmen—or, for that matter, any general consumer of news—might emphasize.

As a frequent interviewee, I have been struck by the inexperience of many reporters and by their lack of preparation, their ignorance of basic economic principles, and what often seems an unnecessarily hostile adversarial attitude. In fact, at the outset of certain interviews I have had the feeling that the interviewer's attitude was one of: "We know you're a crook, and I'm here to find out how and why."

If I were so inclined, I might also point out that although certain pious press litanies tend to emphasize "the people's right to know," the fact is that the primary objective of news organizations—like any private enterprise—is to make a profit.

Moreover, to put some reverse spin on a charge that the media routinely make about my own industry, I might also point to the monopolistic nature of these media profit-making enterprises. As you may know, there are some twenty major oil companies, and no one of these companies has more than 7 or 8 percent of the market for petroleum products. In addition, there are about 10,000 other companies engaged in finding and producing oil and gas. But how many national newspapers are there? By my count, I'd say about four. How many national news magazines are there? Three, unless you want to count the *Harvard Lampoon*. And major networks? Just three. Some may not call that monopoly. But others, to use a term that academics are fond of applying to the oil industry, might call it oligopoly.

And, finally, if I were writing here with critical intentions, I might issue a warning. Freedom and responsibility are inseparable. If there is no freedom, there is no need for responsibility. But if people are free, they must by definition be responsible. And this applies to organizations of people, just as it applies to individual citizens. My friends in the electronic media, for instance, are licensed by their nation to practice their craft. But if they do not exercise responsibility in carrying out their tasks, the citizens of our nation will rise up and demand increasingly stringent regulation. And the signs that this may soon happen are already manifold.

Having made these comments, however, let me say that, from a business perspective, there seem to have been distinct improvements in relations between journalists and the business community. In fact, over the past several years, I have been most impressed with the increased resources which the media — and especially the print media — are committing to business coverage. This is certainly the case, for instance, with the two major newspapers in my own city of Chicago.

I am not presenting my views to pick a fight — although, I must admit, I do hope to stir up just a bit of controversy. The essayist E. B. White once noted that our nation is "a country that was born out of controversy — a country that wrote controversy into its Constitution and set up its legislative bodies on the theory of controversy, that established its free press in the belief that controversy is vital to information, and that created a system of justice of which controversy is the heart and soul."

That, I believe, says it all. I realize that my remarks may sound controversial. But without controversy, there can be no debate. And without debate, there can be no true freedom. However, in order to carry out a meaningful debate, the public must not only be aroused, but informed. And this can happen only when all the facts are laid on the table and all points of view are fully aired. And that, I submit, is the ultimate responsibility of all journalists.

Hypothetical Case Study

ROBERT SCHMUHL

Michael Miller is a prize-winning investigative reporter for the *Daily Sun*, a financially troubled, family-owned newspaper in the capital city of a midwestern state. The *Daily Sun*, which has a tradition of editorially supporting liberal political candidates and causes, is struggling to survive against the *Morning Times*, the flagship paper of Cooper Newspapers, a group of thirty-five newspapers. The editorial policy of the *Morning Times* and the other Cooper newspapers reflects the thinking and convictions of Charles Cooper, one of the country's most prominent conservatives. Contrasting editorial stances notwithstanding, both newspapers have excellent reputations for doing in-depth, investigative stories.

In an effort to promote Miller's journalistic reputation and to enhance the image of the *Daily Sun*, Miller also regularly appears on WCAP-TV with broadcast reports of the stories he does for the *Daily Sun*. Miller, a veteran print reporter who has some suspicions about television news, has an agreement with the *Daily Sun* and WCAP-TV that he will broadcast only material that he has already prepared for his newspaper. During the first six months, his reports, a popular feature on WCAP, have created more interest in the *Daily Sun* and have halted the decline in the paper's circulation. Realizing the popularity and potential of Miller's work, the *Morning Times* has recently made an offer to the reporter that would give him a sizable increase in his salary. Miller has told the editor of the *Morning Times* that he is content at the *Daily Sun*, but that he will consider the proposition.

Miller's new-found celebrity as a television personality has made it increasingly difficult for him to go out in public without being stopped by people who want to discuss a story or converse about topics large and small. Although he at first felt flattered by the amount of attention paid to him, he now considers it something of a burden, especially when people intrude on him and his family when they go to a restaurant or a movie.

In late October, a little more than two weeks before the general election for statehouse offices, including the governor's seat, Miller decided to take his family to an out-of-the-way, out-of-state resort, about 150 miles from the capital, for a weekend. Miller had done some background reporting on the major candidates, but he was not involved in the day-to-day coverage of the campaign. At dinner that Saturday night at the resort's restaurant, Miller was surprised to see William White, one of Governor John Mallory's administrative assistants, along with a woman, who, Miller knew, wasn't White's wife and another couple. White did not see Miller enter the restaurant, and White and the three people with him left shortly thereafter.

Miller did not mention seeing White, but, during dinner, his thoughts remained on the governor's assistant. White enjoyed a reputation similar to the three other chief aides to the governor: He was considered a conscientious and serious assistant, who always found time to talk with reporters and to representatives of interest groups. Governor Mallory set the tone for an open administration, and, throughout his first term, there had been no hint of scandal. There had, in fact, been very little gossip about the governor and his staff. Miller had always thought that the public image projected by Mallory and his people represented the reality of the way in which the administration conducted its public affairs.

Seeing White piqued Miller's interest. The reporter had no intention of writing an article about how an assistant to the governor had spent a weekend. However, Miller wanted to learn more about White and to find out who the other people were. After dinner, Miller stopped by the resort's main desk and asked for the room number of William White. He was told that there was no William White registered at the resort.

The next morning Miller did not see White at breakfast. While leaving the restaurant, however, Miller did see White and the three other people loading their bags into a car at the resort's main entrance. Miller waited until the car was almost ready to leave. He then approached to take note of its license number. He could tell from the tag that the car was registered in a county about sixty-five miles from the capital.

When Miller returned to work Monday morning, he called a source at the state police department to check on the license number. The car was registered to a Glen Johnson of Mapleville. The name meant nothing to Miller, so he called the Mapleville Chamber of Commerce. On the pretense of being a former classmate of Johnson, Miller asked if anyone at the Chamber knew where Johnson might work. The secretary hesitated, saying it would be better to call Johnson's home, but Miller explained that there had been no answer there and that he wanted to reach him right away. The secretary relented, giving Miller the phone number of Wilson Construction Company, where Johnson was the treasurer.

Miller recalled that he had just recently heard of Wilson Construction Company in regard to a situation which he couldn't bring to mind. He asked Susan Wallace, the regional editor of the *Daily Sun*, if she knew anything about the firm. She replied: "Yes. Wilson received the contract to put in the four-lane highway between here and Mapleville. They started work last summer."

Miller's research that morning revealed that Wilson was the low bidder on the project, much to the surprise of the other, larger construction companies seeking the contract. Wilson, which had previously done little work for the state, won the contract after the job had been bid a second time. According to one statehouse source, "We heard that the Highway Department and the governor's office decided the first bids didn't meet specifications. It was the first time this has happened in several years, but it wasn't a big issue." Miller was told that William White served as the governor's liaison on the project.

In the early afternoon, the reporter found only a few clippings about the job in the newspaper's library. In one article that appeared after the bid was awarded, Harold Wilson, the firm's president, said: "For several years, we have wanted to expand our operations. This project allows us to do that, and it will be a necessary shot-in-the-arm for the economic welfare of this area." In another article, written about the ceremony held when construction started, Governor Mallory praised the initiative of the local company and commented: "The new four-lane highway represents this administration's commitment to safety. In the past, Highway 17 has had one of the highest accident rates in our state. When this project is completed, I hope—and trust—that the public will never again refer to Highway 17 as 'the bloody strip.' "

The possible connection between one of the governor's staff people and an officer of the construction company intrigued Miller. He called a source at the Highway Department to inquire about the project. "That job was top priority to the governor's office," the source remarked. "They wanted to get it going before election day. Bill White kept calling to check about it. He ramrodded it through. Some people here thought he might have moved too fast."

For the next three hours, Miller made calls to contacts throughout state government. From some, he sought information about Wilson Construction Company and its work for the state. From others, he elicited background material about William White. Miller discovered that the construction firm had overcome the initial suspicion about its ability to complete such a major project. The work was on schedule, and the state inspectors were impressed with what had thus far been done. The additional information about White reinforced the picture Miller already had of the governor's assistant. A couple of sources mentioned that White, of late, seemed less congenial and more testy, but they suggested that the close re-election campaign against Thomas Harris had made several people around Governor Mallory more pressured and irritable. Harris, a fundamentalist preacher-turned-politician, who appealed to voters' fears and emotions, advocated the dismantling of most of the state programs initiated by Mallory and his two predecessors. Harris was editorially supported by the *Morning Times* and other Cooper newspapers in the state. Mallory had been defended and backed by the *Daily Sun* since his first gubernatorial campaign and throughout his first term.

Late Monday afternoon, Miller called Glen Johnson at Wilson Construction Company. The reporter said he was interested in doing an article on the highway project. Johnson suggested that Miller consult the project engineer regarding a progress report. When Miller mentioned having seen Johnson and White at the resort the previous day, Johnson said, "How I spend a weekend is a private matter" and hung up.

Miller knew Johnson would contact White, and the reporter debated with himself whether he should try to reach White first. He decided to wait and to review the information he had thus far collected with Robert Powell, the editor of the *Daily Sun*. Powell, who had strongly supported Miller's investigative work, urged caution in proceeding with the story. "I'm not sure there's enough here," Powell said. "Find out more about White's relationship to Johnson and Wilson Construction. Right now all you really have is White being caught away from home."

The next morning Miller inspected the bids for the highway project. He discovered that Wilson Construction had not submitted a bid when the project was first advertised. In the early afternoon, he decided to confront White in his office. The receptionist said that Mr. White was ill and was not expected in the office that day.

Wednesday morning, during a news conference away from the capital, Governor Mallory announced that, for reasons of "health" and due to "family matters," William White was resigning as his administrative assistant. "I hate to see Bill leave us," the governor said, "but his doctor thinks he needs to slow down. I know how much Bill's family means to him, and I wouldn't want to see anything happen to him or to them."

A resignation so close to the election caused raised eyebrows among the journalists traveling with the governor and those at the statehouse. But attempts to contact White for amplification failed. No reporter went beyond the governor's statement to explain the aide's departure.

When Miller heard the news about White, he surmised that his call to Johnson had triggered the decision. White was afraid and had gone into hiding. The reported tried to reach the governor through both his statehouse office and his campaign headquarters, but he was unsuccessful.

Although he was unable to speak directly with either Mallory or White, Miller felt he had enough background material to write a story that would at least draw into question the governor's announcement of the resignation. Miller discussed his proposed story with Powell. The editor, however, showed little interest. "White's guilty of something," Powell remarked, "but he's gone now. You know that whatever we run will divert attention from the campaign. The mere suggestion of scandal could ruin Mallory's chances. Given what we know now, I don't think that would be fair. Keep working on it — but I doubt that we'll use anything until after the election."

Leaving Powell's office, Miller understood that a story now would suggest wrongdoing, without actually proving wrongdoing. Such a story, however, would correct the resignation statement, as well as begin the process of "smoking out" information about the relationship between White and Wilson Construction. As Miller left work to go home, he debated with himself regarding what to do the next day:

(1) He could take his editor's advice and keep working on the story for possible publication after the election;

(2) He could propose the story to the news director of WCAP. If the station were to accept the idea of its use, he could either try to sell his paper on it a final time or report it exclusively on WCAP.

(3) He could "leak" the background of the story to a few other reporters in the capital in the hope that they could generate interest in the case before the election;

(4) He could accept the offer from the *Morning Times* to become its chief investigative reporter. Given the tight race between Mallory and Harris and the paper's political leanings, the *Morning Times* might be eager to feature its new reporter by printing a story suggesting a possible scandal in the governor's office.

Analysis of the Case Study

LISA SOWLE CAHILL

I do not know whether credit should go to his experience as an editor, his desire not to become the defendant in a lawsuit, or his expertise as an ethical analyst, but Robert Powell of the *Daily Sun* is on target when he tells Michael Miller, "I'm not sure there's enough here," and, in regard to disclosure, "Given what we know now, I don't think that would be fair." Miller should take Powell's advice to pursue the story quietly, reserving publication until his suspicions have graduated to facts. I intend to substantiate this conclusion from the perspective of the philosopher, which may be modified in conversation with journalism's practitioners.

The case study presents Miller as the victim of conflicting loyalties, in the sort of situation which is the meat of all interesting moral discussions. The intricacies of journalistic responsibility suggested by this case will not be grasped adequately, however, if we approach it using only the language of conflicting "rights," e.g., the "right to free speech" (of Michael Miller), the "right to privacy" (of William White and Glen Johnson), and the "right to know" (of the voting public). These rights are, no doubt, important. In fact, the affirmation of such rights is at the heart of the American tradition of civil liberties. Yet I want to suggest that this tradition is inadequate for providing a coherent moral perspective, to the degree that it fails to join the claiming of rights to the fulfillment of duties. Both rights and duties need to be understood in the context of the good of the body politic. I do not mean to offer a utilitarian position, but rather one incorporating the following principles. First, the

111

good of the community is prior to but does not supersede the rights of any individual members; second, individuals have duties to themselves, to one another, and to the whole, for the sake of the fulfillment of which rights exist and are guaranteed; third, the common good is served when the duties are upheld and the rights of all members are protected; and fourth, all members are equally entitled to share in the goods and benefits entailed by the common good. (This last provision is distinct from a requirement that all must have quantitatively equal shares.)

In any account of social justice which begins with the common good, the ethics of journalism (as of other professions) will be understood in terms of correlative rights and duties. Many who spoke at this conference have suggested that the public has a "right to know" which is served by public media. Jeff Greenfield amplifies that observation by adding that we cannot assert a "right to know" without asking, "a right to know what?"* I would say the "right to know" is based on the right of individuals and groups to possess information adequate for the fulfillment of their duties and for the assertion of other rights upon which their abilities to fulfill duties depend. That level of information adequate for the fulfillment of duties is the "what" of the right to know. Relevant to this case, the public is constituted by voters who have a duty to participate responsibly in the process of government and a right to information that facilitates that participation. Misleading disclosure of incomplete "information" by a source presumed by the public to be reliable presents as great a violation of this right as does the concealment of pertinent information.

At the same time, however, a journalist has a "right to free

---

*I have learned much from the journalists who participated in the conference which resulted in this book and have cited some of their comments. These citations are taken from oral presentations during the conference, and, while I believe my transcriptions to be faithful, they have not been verified by my sources.

speech," i.e., to disclose information and even to express considered opinions. This right is derived not only from his or her right to individual autonomy and right to free expression, but also from the public's "right to know." In a sense, the journalist has a *"duty* of free speech" in regard to the disclosure of information in the public interest; he or she also has a duty to meet this responsibility according to commonly accepted standards of accuracy and reliability. (A distinction can be made between a publication whose policy and practice is to take an explicit advocacy position toward a social, political, or moral point of view and a publication which, while not devoid of perspective, represents itself as aspiring to inform the public objectively.)

Finally, individuals and groups have *prima facie* (presumptive) rights to autonomous self-determination, to freedom from interference in the pursuit of their own welfare and in the fulfillment of their duties (e.g., those entailed by professional roles) in ways which they judge appropriate. These rights are overridden justifiably only when individuals and groups choose to act on them in ways which demonstrably impinge on the rights of others or on the common good. The limits on individual self-determination imposed by the common good increase as the duties of an individual approach a public trust.

A key question in the case study is whether Miller possesses against White and Johnson enough information to furnish a credible claim that they (and Mallory?) are choosing to act out their public and professional roles in ways which endanger the common good and whether that danger is great enough to outweigh their (and Mallory's) right to privacy. The necessity of choosing a concrete path of action, after weighing ambiguous evidence, and predicting what is likely to occur as a result of that choice calls for the exercise of the virtue of prudence, which is always necessary in carrying the moral agent successfully from principle to action. As Edwin Newman tells us, "Journalism is, to say the least, not an exact science." The measuring of the rights of possibly guilty individuals against the common good requires a prudential judgment of a sort endemic to journalism. I think (as a nonspecialist, granted) that a prudent judgment about the facts as we have them is that they do not add up to a threat to the common good warranting publication of Miller's story.

Miller's suspicions were aroused intitially by observing White and three other persons in a restaurant. The woman who appeared to be White's companion was not his wife; the other couple turned out to be an officer of the Wilson Construction Company and, apparently, his wife. Miller's attempts to gather more information directly from White and Johnson were met by evasion. Miller was unable to obtain from the associates of either of the men more than circumstantial evidence about an improper relation between the two. While their relationship appears to have involved wrongdoing in the assignment of the highway contract, the situation is, at least, open to other interpretations. For instance, White might be involved in an extramarital affair, which he is anxious to conceal, not only from the public eye, but more especially from his wife. After all, "health" and "family matters" were cited as reasons for his resignation. His acquaintance with Johnson may be a social one, which began as (licit) cooperation in the construction project; Johnson may be willing to help White conceal the relationship with the woman who was not his wife. This, or possibly even another hypothesis, may amount to a coherent construal of "the facts." The fact that Wilson Construction submitted a bid on the project only during a resolicitation of bids is incriminating only if special state or local laws preclude a contractor from so doing unless he or she has participated in the first round of bids. There is no firm indication that Wilson Construction was given privileged bid information. The possibility that the company was able to submit a winning bid independently was supported by the firm's ability to carry out the project successfully to date. Miller should be wary of a tendency of which Greenfield warns: "Journalists like to think of themselves as *avengers* of some sort," presumably in defense of the public good.

Beside the fact that there exists reasonable, if not considerable, doubt about White's guilt, the impact on the common good of any actual wrongdoing on his part will be lessened because he already has resigned his position and because Governor Mallory's administration appears generally untainted by corruption. Miller's obligation to publicize the association of Johnson and White decreases proportionately. It is also relevant to Miller's decision to publicize or not to publicize the story that resorting to the media available for its release would not be conducive to educating the voters in a truthful, balanced, non-inflammatory manner; it could, rather, incite the public to rash conclusions.

Some consideration in the decision ought to be given to Miller's loyalty to the *Daily Sun*, especially since that loyalty has taken the form of a promise not to release a story on WCAP before it has been published in the newspaper. Although I take promise-keeping to be a *prima facie* duty which, in principle, can be overridden by weightier considerations (e.g., substantial danger to the common good), such considerations seem not to exist here. Judging by the case description, the enhancement of his own reputation, and possibly that of his paper, seems to be one of Miller's prime motives. The aggrandizement of Miller, the *Daily Sun*, or even of Mallory, is a consequence to be promoted only after considerations of justice to all affected have been met (unless one adopts as one's philosophical vantage point egoistic hedonism or possibly utilitarianism). Most dishonesty in reporting, Georgie Anne Geyer points out to us, occurs because of the "careerism" of reporters "who want to make a very quick name for themselves." This is a danger greater than ideology.

There is a final factor in the case about which I admit some perplexity. That is the means by which Miller obtained information. Miller identified Johnson's place of employment by falsely representing himself in a call to the Chamber of Commerce; he also obtained information from what the author of the case refers to as "sources," though whether the latter have disclosed information improperly is not clear. Lying, like breaking promises, is morally reprehensible, unless done for sufficiently serious reasons; the sufficiency of one's reasons must be determined partly in reference to one's circumstances. It is not obvious that the fact that Miller's "interest" was "piqued" provides a sufficient moral warrant for the series of actions, including dishonest ones, which follows. The morality of how Miller uses the information that he obtains, however, can be distinguished from that of how he gets it.

The preferred among Miller's final options is to rely on the experience of his editor and refrain from incriminating White (and, by extension, Mallory's administration) until reliable evidence is available. The alternative which ranks next is to attempt to force Powell to pick up the story by generating the interest of competing papers. By so doing, Miller would avoid direct violation of his contract with the *Daily Sun* and avoid exploitation of the scandalous aspects of the story. Failing that, it would be preferable to release the story to WCAP than to the *Morning Times*, because this would allow Miller to renew his offer to his own paper. To become the chief investigative reporter for the *Morning Times* represents not only a clear "sell-out" of Miller's loyalty to the *Daily Sun* and to his own presumably liberal political convictions, but also of his responsibility as a journalist to inform the public honestly and as objectively as possible and to place the social duties of his profession above personal gain.

In assessing this case, we repeatedly run up against the relation between fact and value, which plagues and perplexes the ethicist and the journalist, along with practitioners of other human sciences. It has been noted frequently that "facts" are available today in overwhelming quantities, due to new technologies of communication. Elie Abel aptly cites the Hutchins Commission's *A Free and Responsible Press*, to the effect that it is part of the responsibility of journalism to supply facts within a context which gives them meaning. Max Lerner accentuates the difficulty of that task by telling us, "The meanings don't come ready-made. You have to sweat for them." Yet, on the other hand, Lerner adduces Max Weber's distinction between fact and value only to remind us that, after all, there is no "objectivity" of the data, devoid of interpretation. The very categories and principles which enable the human mind to observe and organize data already endue them with significance. It thus appears that the journalist will be presented perpetually with a situation in which the presentation of "facts" is never divorced from evaluation, but *truthful* evaluation or the elaboration of an *adequate* context is a very tough and very serious business.

To return to the case at hand, I am skeptical about whether the reporter can "just present facts" in this case and disclaim responsibility for the impression of wrongdoing that the public is likely to receive. To present certain facts (the restaurant dinner, the phone call, the resignation) in association with one another would be to suggest that their proper interpretation involves a causal relationship among them. In order to justify publication of the story, Miller needs a better understanding of what the "facts" are, and, following partly from that, more competence to indicate, in regard to those facts, an appropriate context.

Analysis of the Case Study

REV. EDWARD A. MALLOY, C.S.C.

Perhaps the best way to comprehend the collective self-understanding of the members of a given profession is to search for their internal models of heroic public service. In print and broadcast journalism a number of alternatives come to mind: (1) the muckraking exposer of governmental venality and corporate abuse, (2) the cosmopolitan pundit capable of instantaneous interpretation of major events, (3) the aggressive interrogator of the powerful and pretentious, and (4) the savvy ex-practitioner of political, economic, legal, or educational leadership. What each of these images has in common is the potential for focusing the otherwise dissipated and variegated energies of the whole profession.

In the post-Watergate, Korea-gate era, the model of the investigative reporter has emerged as a publicly respected form of media involvement in, and responsibility for, the broader context of social communication. Especially in a democratic polity, the right to free speech and to a free press is presumed to be somehow related to access to the truth — that level of truth essential for informed public opinion and reasonable voter participation.

The issues raised by the hypothetical case under discussion are best viewed within this framework. For the presumption in the description of Michael Miller's alternatives is that his choices are guided by some higher set of purposes that should not be called into question. Since the citizenry at large has probably been misserved by elected officials, it is his duty to bring the information to the public forum in such a fashion that the commonweal is served. The only question is *how* to achieve this goal, not *whether* it needs to be done.

In order to examine this premise further, let us review the details of the case as described. The first important factor concerns the *origin* of his knowledge of the possible highway construction scandal. Presumably, investigative reporters are perpetually alert for situations of compromise. Like police officers who are armed even while off duty, or physicians who are prepared to render aid in an emergency situation, such reporters must possess a nose for the news, an instinct for the unsavory, the malicious, and the false. Miller began his involvement with the case while on vacation with his family. Requiring no approbation from his editor, he begins almost spontaneously to pursue the leads as they present themselves to his consciousness. His later dilemma is precipitated by this reportorial sixth sense, from which he seemingly cannot disengage even when he is not on assignment.

The first point of ethical difficulty springs from the self-assigned nature of Miller's role in the case. What distinguishes an investigative reporter from a town-tattle, a gossip, a rumormonger? By the nature of his or her job description, is such a person predisposed to interpret appearances in the worst possible light? What public mandate lies behind such access to the press and to the airwaves? Is there a kind of skill that a particular reporter can hone from case to case that dovetails adequately with the fame and public confidence that success in the field often entails?

A second factor meriting consideration is the *methods* employed by Miller in the gathering of evidence. His initial encounter with William White, Glen Johnson, and the others is accidental. However, from then on, he observes, inquires, makes contacts, and strings together a set of disparate bits of information into an increasingly plausible scenario. In a sense, no one's right to privacy has been legally violated. Yet, at the same time, there has been no opportunity for direct response to the emerging charges by those who may be implicated. The greatest constraint on further exploration of the potential malfeasance is the short period remaining before the election. Miller is a solitary agent (in fact and prob-

ably by personal desire as well). He sees his charge as bringing the matter to public attention. Nevertheless, one can
ask whether his resources are adequate to the task he has
assumed.

In classical ethical discussion of personal honor and good
name, the distinction is drawn between *detraction* (revealing
the true faults of our neighbor without sufficient warrant)
and *calumny* or *slander* (concocting a false accusation against
our neighbor in order to damage his or her reputation).
Miller has no reason to engage in calumny (except perhaps if
he switches newspapers and wishes to appeal to the political
allegiances of his new bosses). In regard to detraction, there
are two areas of doubt—whether a true offense has been discovered and whether (if it has) there is sufficient reason to
reveal it. Miller's methods of fact collection seem seriously de-
ficient (i.e., circumstantial, rushed, one-sided, without full
documentary evidence) and, therefore, the reliability of his
conclusions are also suspect. Insofar as sufficient proof is miss-
ing, there is no warrant to proceed on a course of pre-election
revelation. However, at some point in the future, after further sifting of the evidence and an opportunity for response
from those implicated, the level of seriousness of the charges
could warrant the attempt to provoke a judicial inquiry.

A third and final factor that figures prominently in the
case is the *connection between professional responsibility and
career advancement*. Miller is being wooed by a rival
newspaper. His television appearances have made him a
recognizable media figure in the local community. Up to
now he has built his broadcast material around his previous
writing in the *Daily Sun*. The transition from one mode of
communication to the other has been controlled by the somewhat slower time frame of the newspaper business. From his
point of view, as he explores his options, all of these factors
are relevant to a proper decision.

There are several interlocking elements in this configura-
tion which must be unpacked. First, there is the obvious matter of *motivation*. Miller will have a difficult time sorting out

to what extent he is prompted by economic, status, fame, or community-service considerations. The breaking of a major case of civic impropriety will most likely lead to a pay raise, bidding for his services, and other such rewards. In addition, the ratings for his television reports will probably improve and offer a significant alternative for career development. While his motives may not have to be "pure" in the sense of unmixed, they should be consistent enough to avoid the traps that spring from self-deception.

Second, there is the reality of *media competition*. The two newspapers are struggling to appeal to the same market, yet they are guided by contrary political philosophies. Furthermore, they must cultivate a reading audience of sufficient size to counteract the immediacy and pizzazz of the evening news on radio and television. Miller can be pictured as a pawn in a complex process in which the ownership and editorial staff of the two papers are as interested in maximizing readership, and therefore profits, as they are in the moral issues involved in a rigged highway bid.

Third, there is the question of *peer review*. It seems, in the way the case is presented, that the only advisory relationship that concretely affects the decision-making is that between the reporter and the editor. But in cases like this, there would seem to be need for a set of operative guidelines by which investigative reporters could recognize the limits of their competence, as well as the courage and gumption required for their effective participation in safeguarding the well-being of the overall community. How much evidence is enough? Who should cross-check or corroborate the details? What recourse should the accused have to defend their reputations? How much response should be cultivated by other reporters and commentators?

In summary, I have offered an analysis of the "Hypothetical Case Study" which has stressed the role of the investigative reporter as a respected representative of some of the best moral ideals of print and broadcast journalism in general. There are good reasons, I think, for calling into question the unexamined assumptions upon which Michael Miller's claim is made. This case illustrates some of the difficulties endemic in such an enterprise. There may be a few geniuses capable of performing this role with discretion, valor, fairness, and humility. But Michael Miller's claim requires proof, rather than presumption.

Analysis of the Case Study

REV. OLIVER F. WILLIAMS, C.S.C.

As I read about the struggle of Michael Miller of the *Daily Sun*, I was reminded of a comment attributed to the late A. J. Liebling, former writer for the *New Yorker*. He described the order of merit for members of his field as follows: (1) The reporter, who writes what he sees; (2) The interpretive reporter, who writes what he sees and what he construes to be its meaning; (3) The expert, who writes what he construes to be the meaning of what he hasn't seen.

In a serious vein, I take it that the key issue is that Miller is caught in a dilemma: *How to balance the public's right to know with the need to protect innocent people*. If Miller runs the story as he now has it, many readers are likely to conclude that William White, as an agent of Governor John Mallory, acted improperly in his dealings with Glen Johnson, an officer of Wilson Construction Company. While there is not solid evidence of impropriety, there is enough, in the words of Miller, "to suggest wrongdoing without actually proving wrongdoing." Reputations could be harmed, and political careers could be ruined.

In favor of running the story is the argument advanced by Miller that the news coverage would "begin the process of 'smoking out' information about the relationship between White and Wilson Construction." This sort of argument stems from the heart of the genius of the idea of the free press. The First Amendment of the Constitution of the United States states that "Congress shall make no law . . . abridging the freedom of speech, or of the press." According to some, implied in this Amendment is the judgment that the value of a free press is so important for a wholesome and truthful community that mistakes and even sloppy journalism can be tolerated. The community can put up with hacks because, once in a while, even they may expose some important evils or reveal crucial truths to the public.

It is instructive to compare societal expectations for the doctor and the journalist. A doctor is constrained by a fairly detailed code of medical ethics, much of which has the force of law. A journalist, however, is given much more freedom to pursue his or her work, and mistakes are not considered as seriously. As one writer put it, "We outlaw quacks, but protect hacks." People in the public eye have difficulty seeking a legal remedy for libel, the theory being that they can bring their case to the press and make their rebuttal in the media. This is the modern-day version of Jefferson's vision of the salutary workings of a free marketplace of ideas.

To be sure, the Jeffersonian ideal makes no claim that the journalist is incapable of injuring persons and the community. *New York Times* columnist James Reston stated the matter well, if with some humor: "The doctor affects the physical well-being of his patients; the reporter affects the mental well-being of his readers. . . . Like the doctor, he has the opportunity to poison them, and the main difference, it seems to me, is merely that the reporter can poison more of them quicker than the doctor." The argument for allowing this potential "poisoning" in the community is based on a moral judgment of a utilitarian sort. In brief, utilitarians say that an action should be morally assessed on the basis of the aggregate social benefits and aggregate social costs involved with the action. Thus, in our case, Miller can marshal an argument for running the story and "smoking out" more information; the potential benefits (arriving at the truth of the matter and perhaps exposing corruption) more than justify the likely costs (the reputations of some innocent people). The greatest good for the greatest number would seem to justify running the story. Since the *end* of journalism—the pursuit of truth for a wholesome community—is so essential, the *means* are given relatively free reign.

Does the *end* justify the *means?* There surely are instances in the moral life when many would judge that it does.[1] For example, Protestant leader Dietrich Bonhoeffer plotted to assassinate Adolph Hitler, and many were convinced that the *end*, that is, the probable consequences, justified the *means,* deception. Given the enormous evil that Hitler was responsible for over the land, the possibility of a new leader who would be more humane more than justified the means, according to many.

Miller is searching for an answer to whether the end, truth in a wholesome community, justifies the means, "smoking out" — that is, running the story that may harm innocent persons. As the courts in the United States have noted, the intent was never to absolutize freedom of the press. According to the law, citizens have other rights which may clash, and Miller perceives the claims in conflict. Even when the citizens are public figures, responsible journalists will think twice before writing potentially injurious stories. That Miller's dilemma is a real one is born out by a recent article in the *New York Times* discussing the story of the "allegations that several unidentified congressmen had engaged in homosexual activity with teen-age congressional pages." The story was reported by CBS News the evening of June 30, 1982, although reporters had the allegations in early January. It was only when the Federal Bureau of Investigation officially began an inquiry into the situation that CBS ran the story.

Howard Stringer, executive producer of "CBS Evening News," summed up the rationale:

> We had a lot of information for several weeks before we aired the story, including the allegations from the pages; if anything, we were ultracautious. We wanted to wait for some sense that it was being taken seriously elsewhere. When the F.B.I. took the charges seriously enough to launch a full-fledged investigation, then we went ahead and reported on them. (The *New York Times*, Sept. 8, 1982).

Milton Coleman of the *Washington Post* commented on the same story:

You bend over backwards to check a story, but the system isn't foolproof . . . . To a certain degree you print what people tell you. In a case like this, you didn't want to put a cloud over someone's head without sound evidence, but you couldn't totally ignore the story, either.

As an ethicist, I am troubled that the "smoking out" philosophy seems to carry so much legitimacy in journalism, or more precisely, that a utilitarian ethic (the greatest good for the greatest number) is given so much weight in assessing the rightness or wrongness of running a story. I believe Miller must make his decision of whether to run the story by making the difficult judgment of the probable consequences of bringing this matter to the public. Aside from utilitarian standards, he must consider rights (whose rights are at stake and can they be denied?) and justice (are the benefits and burdens going to be fairly distibuted?). The truth may come to light, but at too high a cost.

The "smoking out" approach assumes that a journalist need not have a conscious care for the common good, but rather that simply by pursuing his calling, seeking and writing the truth as it can best be discerned and letting the chips fall where they may, the common good will be enhanced. The "smoking out" approach to journalism and this way of interpreting the First Amendment has an interesting parallel in economics. Adam Smith's doctrine of the "hidden hand" assumed that if each person pursued his or her self-interest, then the common good would be enhanced. Smith believed that a good *end*—a society where people could have the goods and services to lead a humane life—could be achieved by each person seeking his or her own particular good (a market economy). An acquisitive economy, where people actively seek profits, was the means to a humane society. Smith never assumed that we would, or that we should, become an acquisitive society; he never assumed that the profit motive was good in itself—it was only a means to a good end. Many commentators have noted that Smith assumed that compassion, fairness, and integrity would be prevalent in the society and, therefore, the acquisitive economy would never degenerate into an acquisitive society. For Smith, it was crucial that most people in the society espoused humane values; otherwise the market mechanism would not work.[2]

Similarly, I would argue that for the First Amendment — free press dynamic to serve the community well, the journalist must not only be accurate, but also fair, and, especially, *compassionate*. In justice, the journalist must have a conscious care for the common good and assess the probable consequences of writing a story.

Many commentators have noted that Adam Smith believed in God's providence, but that he took too naive and simple a view on the matter. Smith assumed that God works to transform self-interested behavior to a salutary end for the common good. Smith seemed to think that God would override human freedom and make things come out right in spite of bad judgment. It is clear today that all in business must take conscious care for the common good. Pollution control, maintaining the beauty of the land, and so on, need conscious care. We must make God's work our work. Only our free decisions can make the world a more humane place.[3]

In this case, I would side with Robert Powell, "I'm not sure there's enough here." I would not run the story until more facts are available and the probable consequences can be assessed accurately.

NOTES

1. For further discussion see Oliver F. Williams, "Business Ethics: A Trojan Horse," *California Management Review* 24 (Summer 1982), 14-24.

2. See Oliver F. Williams and John W. Houck, eds., *The Judeo-Christian Vision and the Modern Business Corporation* (Notre Dame, Ind.: University of Notre Dame Press, 1982).

3. See Oliver F. Williams, "Christian Formation for Corporate Life," *Theology Today* 36 (October 1979), 347-352.

Analysis of the Case Study

JOHN G. CRAIG, JR.

I will deal with the four options that Miller believed he faced and then mention in passing several other ethical questions that are part of this case.

Option 1. Miller should take his editor's advice and keep working on the story, but there ought also to be some story in the paper dealing with what the *Daily Sun* knows. Preferably the resignation story itself should have included some of this information, though, from the case, one concluded that it did not.

The *Sun* should report that White resigned two days after a reporter for the newspaper attempted to ask him about the nature of his relationship with an officer of the Wilson Construction Company, which has a large highway contract with the state.

The story should be short. It should not have prominent display. It should make clear that the highway department says that the contract is being fulfilled satisfactorily by Wilson.

The story should include the fact that White and Johnson were together for the weekend at the resort. It should not deal with their female companions, but it should make it clear in its chronology — and chronology is the key to the story at this time — that it was when the reporter saw the two men at dinner that this story began and that, when asked about the meeting, Johnson had said, "How I spend a weekend is a private matter."

128

The story should avoid any hint of impropriety as far as the bidding and re-bidding are concerned, as well as avoiding White's role as a ramrod in getting the contract going. The facts in the case do not justify mention of these matters in the story; to do so would suggest impropriety where none is yet known to exist.

The fact that the story might have an effect on the outcome of the election is central to the decision to publish. It is better to get out pertinent information before the election than afterward. If this develops into a full-blown scandal as the result of the story, the public will have been well served. If nothing comes of it, the public also will have been well served.

Publication could damage the newspaper's choice for governor and put into office a man that the newspaper believes could cause harm to the state. That should not deter it from pursuing the facts. Management of the news columns to further the owner's political or social goals is a legitimate exercise only to the extent that it does not suppress significant information.

I would digress here for a moment, however, to observe that blatant partisanship in the news columns is not an ethical question; it is a business question. An editor and/or owner tries to publish information that is complete and accurate, because experience has shown that this is the most effective way to gain the trust of one's readers and to keep them as customers. A publisher trades off, in such matters, the frustration of not being able to further, without restraint, his political and social interests in favor of the financial strength that comes from the consistent publication of news in a straightforward and evenhanded manner.

There are those who would argue that publishers attempt to be "fair" for other reasons, with the "public service" function of the news business in American society being most often cited as an explanation. I approach such statements with a great deal of caution because, in a heterogeneous society such as ours, it is not always obvious where the "public interest" lies. One man's self-evident truth is another's obvious falsehood.

Journalism is, in my opinion, still a very individual enterprise and best kept that way, with practitioners pursuing their craft to the best of their ability, given their best judgment—and the best judgment of the particular news organization to which they are attached—of what the best standards of their craft are and what the interests of their public demand. I am not partisan and would argue that the *Sun* not be partisan, either, because it is consistent with what I believe to be the most effective approach to daily newspaper journalism, because it is consistent with my professional values, if you wish, and not because the *Sun* or any other newspaper is under any ethical obligation to so behave.

Now, back to the business at hand. White's social activities are not, at this stage, a legitimate subject of public concern. White has a right to privacy about the nature of his relationship, if any, with the "other woman." For that reason, I keep her out of the story, even though the governor, should he feel compelled to say more about this matter once the newspaper has published its account, may make her a public figure by mentioning her relationship with White.

White's social relationship with Johnson is a legitimate subject of public concern because White is a public figure and his public work has involved matters that could involve the proprietary interests of both Johnson and the public. But fairness demands that nothing be done beyond stating the fact of that relationship and the events that followed, once the reporter started asking questions.

I find Miller's decision not to talk to White very peculiar. Professional, if not ethical, considerations argue for contacting a subject before he has had time to "get his story straight." It is almost as if Miller wanted to be sure to alert White to pending trouble that he called Johnson first. Any reporter or editor worth his salt would have been in White's office (and the governor's for that matter) for an on-the-record, tape-recorded conversation once the Wilson relationship had been established.

For reasons that are obvious, given the arguments above, Editor Powell's contention that "You know whatever we run will divert attention away from the campaign" is indefensible. He should be severely reprimanded, at the least, for leadership on this story that, to be charitable in the extreme, could be described as weak.

Option 2. If Miller has decided he wants to make his career in TV news at WCAP and forget newspapering, he should share the story with the news director of WCAP. If he has not, he should keep his mouth shut.

Trying to blackmail one's editor into doing what he is otherwise disinclined to do is not unknown in the news business, but the risks of such behavior to interpersonal relationships and the nature of life within the related organization are obvious.

As for the WCAP news director, if he were a wise man he would not accept Miller's story unless Miller had agreed first to terminate his employment at the *Sun*. Though the temptations would be great, the news director also should not put other people in his organization on the story until the nature of Miller's relationship with WCAP and the *Daily Sun* is clear.

Option 3. There is no justifiable reason for leaking the story. If Miller's relationship with his editor and his newspaper has been unilaterally terminated by the editor's behavior, in Miller's opinion, Miller has another, more effective and professionally defensible, option available to him. Go someplace else, either to WCAP or the *Morning Times*.

Getting other reporters or friends to do your dirty work is certainly not unknown in journalism, but that does not make it defensible. Similarly, while it may be true that once a story is "out" it is often taken up by media that would not have initiated its circulation, that does not justify Miller's violating his professional relationship with his employer.

Also, as long as the "social contract" between Miller and the newspaper is in force, the story is not Miller's to leak. It belongs to both him and the newspaper, once he has discussed it with his editor. This is primarily a professional matter, but under certain circumstances it could become a proprietary one.

I would make another parenthetical observation here. Sharing a story with others off the record or "shopping a story around" is, if not widespread, not unknown today. It is very common for news organizations, including my own, to print stories initiated by others that include subject matter or take an approach that they would not have included had they developed the story themselves. Once the material is "out," printing it somehow becomes ethically defensible, where, before, it was not. The news itself makes the news, if you will. The way in which the press handled the sexual preference of Spiro Agnew's son and the material produced by *New York Magazine* on John DeLorean are two cases in point. This bothers me.

Option 4. The pertinent question here is whether or not Miller can take his story with him, should he decide to leave the *Daily Sun* and go to the *Morning Times.* I think he can, as long as the editor of the *Daily Sun* is given some warning about what he is about to do. If Miller were to give the story to the *Times* before moving or to use it as an inducement for additional money or position he would be professionally irresponsible.

The same arguments used above on the relationship between the governor's race and the handling of the story should apply to the *Morning Times*, when it comes to how the story is handled. Miller should not do for the *Times* what he would not do for the *Sun*.

Reporters who lose their independence as private contractors and become hired guns also lose their effectiveness. At the same time, as has already been pointed out, when you join a news organization you must realize that stories developed with the aid of that organization's resources are not yours alone.

I would make these additional observations on several tangential matters in the case.

I have no problems with print journalists also going on television. The key ingredient is the nature of the contract between the reporter and his primary employer; in Miller's case it was the *Daily Sun* which found Miller's television broadcasts helpful and therefore permitted them. Another newspaper might not and might prohibit a similar arrangement. Both alternatives seem acceptable to me.

Reporters should not misrepresent themselves. Miller should not have posed as a former classmate of Johnson's when trying to get his home address. He should merely have given his name and asked for the address; if the secretary asked him who his employer was, Miller should have told her.

The key event in this story is the resignation. The newspaper has an obligation to explain it; its customers have a right to expect an explanation of it from the newspaper. Before the resignation the story may have been Miller's; afterward it was not.

Selected Bibliography

Brown, Lee. *The Reluctant Reformation: On Criticizing the Press in America.* New York: David McKay Company, 1974.

Casebier, Allan, and Janet Jinks Casebier, eds. *Social Responsibilities of the Mass Media.* Washington, D.C.: University Press of America, 1978.

Christians, Clifford G., and Catherine L. Covert. *Teaching Ethics in Journalism Education.* Hastings-on-Hudson, N.Y.: The Hastings Center, 1980.

Christians, Clifford G., Kim B. Rotzoll, and Mark Fackler. *Media Ethics: Cases and Moral Reasoning.* New York: Longman, 1983.

The Commission on Freedom of the Press. *A Free and Responsible Press.* Chicago: University of Chicago Press, 1947.

Crawford, Nelson Antrim. *The Ethics of Journalism.* New York: Alfred A. Knopf, 1924.

Flint, Leon Nelson. *The Conscience of the Newspaper: A Case Book in the Principles and Problems of Journalism.* New York: D. Appleton, 1925.

Gerald, James Edward. *The Social Responsibility of the Press.* Minneapolis: University of Minnesota Press, 1963.

Gibbons, William Futhey. *Newspaper Ethics: A Discussion of Good Practice for Journalists.* Ann Arbor, Mich.: Edwards Bros., 1926.

Goodwin, H. Eugene. *Groping for Ethics in Journalism.* Ames: Iowa State University Press, 1983.

Gross, Gerald, ed. *The Responsibility of the Press.* New York: Fleet Publishing Co., 1966.

Haselden, Kyle. *Morality and the Mass Media.* Nashville: Broadman Press, 1968.

Heine, William C. *Journalism Ethics: A Case Book.* London, Ont.: University of Western Ontario Library, 1975.

Henning, Albert F. *Ethics and Practices in Journalism.* New York: R. Long and R. R. Smith, 1932.

Hulteng, John L. *The Messenger's Motives: Ethical Problems of the News Media*. Englewood Cliffs, N. J.: Prentice-Hall, 1976.

_____.*Playing It Straight: A Practical Discussion of the Ethical Principles of the American Society of Newspaper Editors*. Chester, Conn.: Globe Pequot Press, 1981.

Johannesen, Richard L. *Ethics in Human Communication*. Columbus, Ohio: Charles E. Merrill, 1975.

Lahey, Thomas Aquinas, C.S.C. *The Morals of Newspaper Making*. Notre Dame, Ind.: University Press, 1924.

Merrill, John C. *The Imperative of Freedom: A Philosophy of Journalistic Autonomy*. New York: Hastings House, 1974.

Merrill, John C., and Ralph D. Barney, eds. *Ethics and the Press: Readings in Mass Media Morality*. New York: Hastings House, 1975.

Merrill, John C., and S. Jack Odell. *Philosophy and Journalism*. New York: Longman, 1983.

Rivers, William L., et al. *Backtalk: Press Councils in America*. San Francisco: Canfield Press, 1972.

Rivers, William L., Wilbur Schramm, and Clifford C. Christians. *Responsibility in Mass Communication*. 3rd ed. New York: Harper and Row, Publishers, 1980.

Rubin, Bernard, ed. *Questioning Media Ethics*. New York: Praeger Publishers, 1978.

Swain, Bruce M. *Reporters' Ethics*. Ames: Iowa State University Press, 1978.

Thayer, Lee, ed. *Communication: Ethical and Moral Issues*. New York: Gordon and Breach, 1973.

Thayer, Lee, ed. *Ethics, Morality, and the Media: Reflections on American Culture*. New York: Hastings House, 1980.

Yost, Casper S. *The Principles of Journalism*. New York: D. Appleton, 1924.

Contributors

ELIE ABEL, who was dean of Columbia University's Graduate School of Journalism from 1970 to 1979, is the Harry and Norman Chandler Professor of Communication at Stanford University. Before beginning his academic career, he spent a quarter-century in journalism. He served as a national and foreign correspondent for the *New York Times* and as the diplomatic correspondent and London bureau chief for NBC News. His publications include *The Missile Crisis, Roots of Involvement, The U.S. in Asia, 1784-1971* (with Marvin Kalb), *Special Envoy to Churchill and Stalin* (with W. Averell Harriman), and *What's News: The Media in American Society.*

LISA SOWLE CAHILL is an associate professor of theology at Boston College, who specializes in Christian theological ethics, medical ethics, and sexual ethics. She has written articles for the *Journal of Religious Ethics, Religious Studies Review,* the *Journal of Medicine and Philosophy,* and *Theological Studies.* She delivered the 1983 Earl Lectures at the Pacific School of Religion, Berkeley, California. These lectures are to be published as a book by Fortress Press, *Between the Sexes: A Study of Method in Christian Ethics* (1984).

JOHN G. CRAIG, JR., has been editor of the *Pittsburgh Post-Gazette* since 1977. He previously was editor of the *News-Journal* newspapers in Wilmington, Delaware. He has served on the ethics committee of the American Society of Newspaper Editors and is chairman of its press/bar committee.

GEORGIE ANNE GEYER writes a syndicated column on foreign affairs for Universal Press Syndicate. From 1960 to 1975, she was a reporter and foreign correspondent for the *Chicago Daily*

News. Her books include *The New Latins, The New 100 Years' War, The Young Russians,* and *Buying the Night Flight.* She is a frequent participant on such television programs as "Washington Week in Review" and "Meet the Press."

JEFF GREENFIELD is a commentator on media and politics for ABC News and a columnist for Universal Press Syndicate. A former political consultant and media critic for CBS News, he is the author of eight books, including *Television: The First Fifty Years, Playing to Win: An Insider's Guide to Politics,* and *The Real Campaign: How the Media Missed the Story of the 1980 Campaign.*

MAX LERNER, the author and columnist for the Los Angeles Times Syndicate, is the W. Harold and Martha Welch Professor of American Studies at the University of Notre Dame. He previously taught at Sarah Lawrence College, Harvard University, Williams College, Brandeis University, and United States International University. His books include *America as a Civilization, Ideas Are Weapons, Ideas for the Ice Age, The Age of Overkill,* and *Values in Education.*

ROBERT J. McCLOSKEY, the ombudsman of the *Washington Post,* was a career foreign service officer for more than twenty-five years until his retirement in 1981. From 1957 until 1973, he served in several capacities in the State Department's Bureau of Public Affairs, including ten years as official press spokesman. He subsequently served as Ambassador to Cyprus, to the Netherlands, to Greece, and as Assistant Secretary of State for Congressional Relations.

REV. EDWARD A. MALLOY, C.S.C., is associate provost and associate professor of theology at the University of Notre Dame. He is the author of several books and articles about contemporary ethics, including *Homosexuality and the Christian Way of Life* and *The Ethics of Law Enforcement and Criminal Punishment.*

EDWIN NEWMAN has been a correspondent, critic, and commentator for NBC News since 1952. He has reported from thirty-five foreign countries, anchored many "instant news specials," and served as the reporter on many network documentaries. A watchdog of English usage, he is the author of two popular books on language, *Strictly Speaking: Will America Be the Death of English?* and *A Civil Tongue*. His novel *Sunday Punch* appeared in 1979.

ROBERT SCHMUHL is an assistant professor of American Studies and Communication Arts at the University of Notre Dame. From 1975 to 1980, he was coordinator of the Citizen and the News Project at Indiana University's Poynter Center on American Institutions. He is the editor of *The Classroom and The Newsroom* and has contributed to *The Review of Politics, Style, Journalism Quarterly*, and *National Forum*.

LEONARD SILK is the economics columnist of the *New York Times* and Distinguished Visiting Professor of Economics at Pace University. From 1954 to 1969, he served as economics editor, senior editor, editorial page editor, and chairman of the editorial board of *Business Week*. His books include *Ethics and Profits, The Economists, Economics in Plain English*, and *The American Establishment* (with Mark Silk).

JOHN E. SWEARINGEN was chairman of the board of directors of Standard Oil Company (Indiana) on his retirement in 1983. He spent forty-four years with Standard in various positions and was chief executive officer from 1960 to 1983.

REV. OLIVER F. WILLIAMS, C.S.C., is a theologian and ethicist in the department of management at the University of Notre Dame. An authority on religion and business values, his publications include *The Judeo-Christian Vision and the Modern Corporation, Co-Creation and Capitalism: John Paul II's "Laborem Exercens,"* and *Full Value: Cases in Christian Business Ethics*.